Identity, Power, and Conflict:

Inter-ethnic Perspective of Northern Nigeria Religious Violence

A Holistic Single Case Study

by

Cecilia Iro-Cunningham

ISBN: 978-1-365-58850-1

PublishNation LLC
www.publishnation.net

Dedication

I am dedicating this dissertation to my one and only child, DESTINY ADAEZE CUNNINGHAM, who has stood by me throughout this process. It was all because of you that this began in the first place. You were just three months old when I started my doctoral degree program. Today you are four years old and have turned out to be the most beautiful, intelligent girl I have ever seen. I love you more than words can say baby, and I'm looking forward to better years ahead with you.

Acknowledgments

I would like to acknowledge all those that worked with me in making this project a reality. To my family, especially my brother Patrick Iro who is never tired of listening and standing by me in my doings—God bless you, brother.

Most of all to the ALMGHTY GOD who has directed my steps and given me the ability to achieve far more than I ever thought or asked of Him. Blessed be your name forever.

Table of Contents

List of Tables

List of Figures

Chapter 1

Introduction

Violence in major northern parts of Nigeria has been a recurring event since after the nation's independence and the 1967 Biafran War. Many scholars have analyzed the violence as religiously related between the dominant Muslim Hausa and non-indigenous Christian groups living in the region (Chidi, n.d.; Irobi, 2005; Olu-Adeyemi, 2006). Based on the religious-related analysis, several conflict management options by state and federal governments, as well as international bodies, have been applied without major positive results.

Some of the peace-keeping strategies applied from 1999 to 2013 include the creation of more states, the Inter-Religious Council (NIREC), the Kaduna Peace Declaration, and the recent Interfaith Mediation Center in Kaduna (International Crisis Group, 2010). These groups are intended to help manage misunderstanding and mend damaged relationships between the religious groups. Despite these efforts, violence continues to erupt in the major cities of Northern Nigeria, threatening the stability and safety of the people.

The inability to resolve or manage the violence could be attributed to "wrong diagnosis of an ailment that results to wrong medical prescription" (Olu-Adeyemi, 2006, para. 20). The social and economic implications of the violence cannot be over-emphasized. The accompanying security and economic threats are not only a national problem; it has also attracted international attention for terrorism surveillance.

While Islamic religion happens to be a dominant characteristic of the Northern people of Nigeria, it is also a major distinguishing factor between them and people from other regions of the country.

Like most African countries that experienced the British Colonial administration era, the contemporary nation of Nigeria is composed of different regions with distinct ethnic groups, as well as distinct

1

cultural, religious, and other value systems. Background history of the country indicates the regions were carved from the former Niger River Basin with four distinct ecological zones. The thick rainforest ecological zone inhabited the Igbo speaking groups, while the Northerners and certain parts of the Southerners such as the Nupe, Gwari, and Hausas dwelt in the semi-arid savanna grassland. A majority of the rest of the Southerners were carved from the mangrove and rainforest vegetation (Ejiogu, 2013). These geographical differences influence their cultural values, professions, and political systems.

Culturally, the Igbo regions were mostly traders, and their trading businesses took them to different parts of the regions and other African countries such as Cameroon "to supplement for what they needed but could not raise themselves" (Ejiogu, 2013, p. 655). Their political system revolved around their social groups such as family, age group, village, and clan. They practiced "highly democratic political systems and had no need for large political organizations or centralized institutional structures" (p. 655). This system was not suitable for the British colonial autocratic system, and the people rebelled against them from the onset.

The Northerners comprising the Hausas, Nupes, Gwaris, and others from the upper Niger basin had major features of "conquest and control of people" as synonymous with the semi-arid savanna people (Ejiogu, 2013, p. 656). The open savanna allowed "free movement of other groups and people from their vicinity that exposed them to continual conflicts and warfare" (p. 656). The Islamic religion was introduced to them through the Sarkin rule which is associated with Islamic courts, and with rent paid to the Sarkins. The Sarkins continued to extend their "empire through jihad by conquering other surrounding areas of the north, the Niger basin and the south of Illorin" (p. 656). The Sarkins adopted a centralized, autocratic, feudalist type of ruling system to enable them to preside and administer over their Empire. The British colonial masters under the command of Frederick Lugard formed a coalition with the Fulani Jihad to overthrow and defeat the Sultan (p. 658). The British co-opted the Hausa-Fulani centralized and highly autocratic ruling and applied the system for what became Nigeria as an amalgamated country.

The British continued to rule the nation from different administrative offices of the colony and protectorates instituted in the northern and southern regions even after the 1914 amalgamation (Mustapha, 2004). The Protectorate of Southern Nigeria was divided into Central and Eastern Provinces with west and east of the River Niger (Mustapha, 2004, p. 4). The two groups were later merged to become the Western and Eastern regions in the 1914 amalgamation. However, the British government continued to run the North and South as separate political and administrative entities for their political and financial gains.

Although there were "no unifying policies adopted by the colonial masters," the International Crisis Group (ICG) suggests major infrastructural buildings such as railroads were concentrated in the North and extended to different parts of the country (Mustapha, 2010, p. 5). The railroads helped in transportation of major cash crops cultivated in the North such as groundnuts, yams, and cola nuts to other regions. Most Southern and Eastern businessmen took advantage of the railroads to expand their businesses and later migrated to the region for better living conditions. By "1950 to 1951, about 4 to 5 million of the 31 million Nigerians" were living in major cities of the Northern Nigeria (p. 4). The Northerners under the direction of the British government carved out separate parts of their cities for non-indigenous Northerners (Mustapha, 2004, p. 4; ICG, 2010, p. 5). Non-Northerners were isolated in major northern cities in separated areas known as the sabon-garis (strangers' quarters or native foreigners). The ICG stated that the segregation distinguished the Northerners from other regions living in the area and "provided areas of concentration at each violence" (Mustapha, 2004, p. 5). Sabon-garis are still in existence in major cities of Northern Nigerian today.

The colonial divide-and-rule system continued to conduct its indirect rule system through the local chiefs, caliphates, and the imams that continued to influence localism and regionalizations until the amalgamation period. By 1951, national political parties were formed around regional groups that fought for the domination of their area in federal government and cabinets (ICG, 2010, p. 6). The Northern People's Congress (NPC) was dominated by the Northern Hausa-Fulani people. The Action Group (AG) was dominated by

3

Yorubas from the South while the NCNC (National Council of Nigeria and the Cameroons) were for the Eastern Igbo people.

The purpose for democracy became struggle over domination of federal power rather than getting rid of the colonial foreign administration. Struggle for power resulted in the 1966 military coup and recoup of 1967 that transitioned to the 1967 Biafran War. The 1966 coup that came six years after the country gained its independence from the British colonial rule was asserted to have been carried out by "a number Christian-Igbo soldiers" who were displeased with Northern domination of federal power (ICG, 2010, p. 8). Chinua Achebe countered the report of Igbo military involvement in the coup as "a framed allegation based on the Northerners long resentment for Igbos that were successful in virtually all sectors of commerce, education, arts and politics" (Njoku, 2013, p. 716). In July, 1967, three months after the first coup, another coup succeeded under the leadership of a Christian from the minority north, Yakubu Gowon. "Igbo Nigeria Military officers, especially in Northern Nigeria were rounded up and killed" (p. 716). Igbo civilians were sought from "their homes, offices, places of businesses and hideouts with loudspeakers announcing "The Igbos must go – the infidels must go" while enchantments of "Araba, araba" filled the air (p. 716). The Igbos were killed in the thousands leading to their mass flee back to their regions. Mudimbe (2013) suggests the two coups were "motivated and expressed by competing will of power and interests" (p. 674). A majority of the surviving Igbo groups in Northern Nigeria fled back to their region.

In 1967, the then military governor of the Eastern Region of Nigeria, Lt. Col. Ojukwu, proclaimed the autonomy of the Igbo state. The federal government of Nigeria saw the action as rebellious against the Republic of Nigeria and fought to regain the region back to the federation. The "1967 Biafran war was fought by the Eastern Igbo majority region led by their military governor against the Northern-dominated Federal Government of Nigeria" (Njoku, 2013, p. 717). Atofarati (1992) suggests the major cause of the war was due to "the coup and counter coup staged by the Northern military officers that was intended to revenge against the Easterners and break-up the country" (para. 24). The secession of the Biafran-Igbo-Eastern region under the leadership of Ojukwu and later surrendered

4

to the federal government was reabsorbed into the Nigerian state in 1970.

The war was declared "no victor, no vanquished with a hegemony of once conquered rights vanquished" (Mudimbe, 2013, p. 676). Mudimbe suggests that there was no real closure to the political defeat and that the question of whether a Nigerian state exists still prevails (p. 676). Since then, violence termed as political, religious, or ethnical have never ceased in many parts of Nigeria especially in the major cities of Northern Nigeria. More than a dozen coups took place in Nigeria between 1960 to 1999 with over twenty-eight civil violence events between 1960 to 2010 (Ezeibe, 2009; ICG, 2010, pp. 31-33; Olu-Adeyemi, 2006, pp. 6-7). About twenty of the civil unrests took place in major cities of Kano, Jos, Zaria, and Kaduna of Northern Nigeria over different reasons.

Purpose of the Study

This book based on qualitative case study of the case is relevant and significant for several reasons. First, violence of any type is a global concern. Second, violence in major Northern Nigeria cities has been recurring for over 40 years and has failed all conflict resolution strategies. Continual violence in Northern Nigeria is a threat to the security and economic stability of the nation as well as the world at large because unattended violence can transform to more dangerous consequences.

The study examined the role of inter-ethnic struggles in major Northern Nigeria religious violence. Inter-ethnical conflict continues to be a problem in most African countries that experienced the colonial divide-and-rule system, and its characteristics differ according to societies. To attain the purpose of the study, I analyzed theoretical explanations of colonial divide-and-rule systems through localism and regionalization that transformed to struggle for power and resources amongst Nigerian major regions. The literature brings understanding of how colonial favoritism and inequality in distribution of infrastructure created fear for loss of power and hatred amongst the regions. The creation of political parties along regional and ethnic lines became the framework for local political elites in the manipulation of the masses for political and economic aims. Further theoretical analysis is used to find connection to the 1966/1967 military coups and the Biafran War as ethnically influenced.

Purposeful selection of major cities of Northern Nigeria that include Kano, Kaduna, Jos, and Zaria where violence have been recurring since pre-independence were selected for data collection. Further information for future research in inter-ethnic conflict was provided at the end of the study.

Inter-ethnical conflict continues to be a problem in most African countries that experienced the British Colonial administration. In Nigeria, the merging of about 400 different regions with over 250 different languages, with distinct origins, as well as historical and cultural backgrounds is known to influence conflicts amongst the groups. Violence began to erupt between ethnic groups immediately after the 1960 independence over the struggle for political and economic power which was preceded by the 1966 coup, recoup of 1967, and finally the Biafran War. Violence continued to recur in different parts of Nigeria, especially in the major cities of Northern Nigeria resulting in continual loss of lives and properties. The inability to recognize religion as part of ethnic characteristics that can be manipulated by political elites in justifying their political aims limits resolution strategies for the Northern Nigerian violence.

This case study examined the role of inter-ethnic struggles in the Northern Nigeria religious violence. To this end, the pre-colonial geographical and political background of the regions before the British 1914 amalgamation of the regions was traced. The colonial divide-and-rule system through regionalized administration and the creation of political parties along ethnic lines that influenced struggles for political and economic power amongst the regions were also analyzed.

Human Identity theory which is made up of three themes of Primordialism, Constructivism, and Instrumentalism was applied in analyzing the conflict.Primordialism assumes ethnic identity as inherited by birth or blood connection and is, therefore, fixed. Instrumentalism suggests ethnic identity is regulated by societal institutions like political parties, social clubs, and other group affiliations. Constructivism suggests ethnic identity is influenced through the domination power of colonial masters and therefore, uses colonial experience in explaining the ethnic cleavages. The three themes of Human Identity theory were applied in analyzing how religion as part of ethnic characteristic shapes the identity of people and can be manipulated by local elites in justifying political aims.

Multiple sources of data were collected through structured and unstructured interviews and through the examination of documents from libraries, archives, and secondary sources such as journals and newspapers. Participants for the study were selected through purposeful sampling from cities like Kano, Jos, Kaduna, and Zaria where violence is intense based on the literature review. Open-ended interviews were conducted in social groups' or individual's choice of venue within each site for a two month period for detailed understanding and description of the issue. Similarities of findings were compared to find connection of ethnicity struggles in the Northern Nigeria religious violence or otherwise.

Outlines

This study is divided into five chapters:

Chapter 1 contains the introduction, problem statement, research questions, conceptual framework, historical background, purpose of the study, significance of the study, rational for qualitative study, and the dissertation outline.

Chapter 2 outlines the literature review that covers ethnic theory, ethnic identity, inter-ethnical theories, secession, and the human identity theory themes of primordalism, instrumentalism, and constructivism along with their conceptualization to religion and conflict.

Chapter 3 is the methodological applied; data collection procedures (interviews, non-participant observations, documentation, and reflective journals), data analysis, ethical considerations, validation strategies, and the researcher's role and background.

7

Chapter 4 contains tabulated comparison of case-by-case data analysis from the four sites of study, regional data presentation of records of federal cabinet offices, and military colleges and units disposition from reputable academic journals, newspapers, and archives from 1960 to 2013.

Chapter 5 is a summary of the study that includes the implication of the findings, recommendations, areas for future research, strength and weaknesses, and lessons learned.

Chapter 2

Historical Background of the regions

Research on inter-ethnic violence indicate that colonial manipulation of historical backgrounds, discrimination, and favoritism of certain groups created fear, hatred, and competition over power and resources amongst the groups that contributed to the problem (Blagojevic, 2009; Mustapha, 2004; Wimmer, 1997). Inter-ethnical conflict is known to be common with Third World countries that went through the British colonial administrative system. Heterogeneous societies in most African countries that went through colonial administration experienced inter-ethnic conflicts (Wimmer, 1997, p. 637). Nigeria is described as one of the most heterogeneous countries in the world with over 400 ethnic groups and about 250 linguistic differences (Olu-Adeyemi, 2006). The foundation behind regional conflicts between the Igbo and Hausa ethnic groups can be traced as far back as the 1966/1967 coups and the Biafran War. The Eastern-Igbo dominated region sort secession from the Hausa dominated federal government of Nigeria due to marginalization in political powers and inequality in distribution of resources and infrastructures.

This study assumed that major conflicts in Nigeria including the Northern religious violence is attributed to a struggle for power and economic access between dominant Muslim Hausa and non-indigenous Christian Igbo ethnic groups based on studies from the literature review. Inter-ethnic conflicts continue to be a problem in most African countries that experienced the British colonial administrative system. Colonial divide-and-rule systems segregated regions for their economic gains and security purposes. Regionalizing of political systems, inequality in economic distribution, and use of local leaders encouraged disparity amongst the groups. Regions concentrated on struggle over political and economic power rather than getting rid of the foreign leaders.

Human Identity theory themes of Primordialism, Instrumentalism, and Constructivism are applied in analyzing the influence of colonial structuring, regionalized administration, and creation of political parties along ethnic lines in the Nigerian regional conflicts. The history of chronological events such as the 1966/1967 coups and the Biafran War in which the Igbo dominated the eastern region sort secession from the Hausa dominated federal government due to marginalization and inequality in political power, and distribution of resources is analyzed for foundational description of the study.

Pre-colonial geographical/political history. What is known as the country of Nigeria today was carved out from four different ecological regions of the lower and upper Niger basin with distinct cultural, religious, and political systems. The lower Niger basin was characterized with its mangrove ecological zone that inhabited certain parts of the current Eastern region. These comprise the Ogoni, Ubani, Efik, Ijaw, Kalabari, and other cities known as the Rivers State of today. The people were known as "great watermen, fishermen and traders" prior to the European invasion (Ejiogu, 2013, p. 655). Their political system was structured around several houses and a constitution. The houses were organized according to a hierarchy of fishermen and their slaves who engaged in their trading principals (p. 654). Each had political ranks such as House Heads, Chiefs, and other ranks of chiefs. These "hierarchies had the opportunity of rising from one level to the other" (p. 655). The Ibeno or Ibibios of today's Cross Rivers State, however, practiced the monarchical political system with the legislative, executive, and judicial authorities (p. 655). The highest rank and law making group was the Ekpe group.

The Igbos, Ibibios, Ogoja, and others that make up the Eastern region of Nigeria, mainly dominated by the Igbos, were carved from the thick evergreen rainforest ecological zone. The Igbos were mostly traders and farmers who engaged in agricultural produce for their economic development. The Igbos particularly engaged in "long distance trading" that evolved around the Niger basin and stretched to other nearby African countries such as the Cameroons (Ejiogu, 2013, p. 655). They practiced a village-based democratic type of political system that revolved around their social groups, namely families, village heads, and clans. This type of system

10

clashed with the colonial administrative autocratic system, and they also rebelled against their authorities.

The Southern Yorubas, Binis, Itekiri-Urhobo, and others composing Lagos and the Mid-Western region were from the rainforest ecological zone. The area dominated by the Yorubas relied on "the agency to build and transform monarchical states that transformed into political organizations" (Ejiogu, 2013, p. 655). They practiced a mixture of a monarchical political system with a democratic system. The Yorubas have great respect for elders and societal authorities in their respective town-based kingdoms. They were, however, known to "import foreign practices like adoption, importation of war horses, use of eunuchs and non-eunuch slaves" that were associated with the Northern Nupes (p. 655). These practices enabled them to transform and expand their monarchies far beyond their territories.

The semi-arid savanna grassland of the upper Niger basin comprised the Hausas, the Nupes, Gwari, and other regions of Northern Nigeria. The open savanna and presence of tse-tse flies encouraged free movement of people into and out of the area (Ejiogu, 2013, p. 656). These unhindered movements exposed them to regular conflicts and war with foreigners. They were introduced to the Islamic religion by the Sarkins in the "14th century with talakwas, extensive court system and well equipped standard armies that sustained the government" (p. 656). The practices that came with the autocratic political system included rent payment to the Sarkins, appropriation of properties, labor, and self-abasement ceremonies for men and women (p. 656). They later intermingled and entered into marriage relationships with the Fulani Islamic teachers that migrated to the area. The Northern region expanded their empires through the Jihad war, while relying on highly a centralized autocratic and feudalist political system to maintain their ruling. The British colonial masters under the governance of Frederick Lugard took advantage of the people's warfare, and defeated and killed the last Sultan in 1803 (p. 656). They were later absorbed into the British colonial administration towards the end of the 19th century. Their elders and political system were incorporated into Nigerian administration under Frederick Lugard as the High Commissioner.

11

Frederick Lugard adopted the Hausa-Fulani centralized autocratic Caliphate in the British colonial system with its institutions to achieve their imperial goals (Ejiogu, 2013, p. 658). As the High Commissioner of Northern Nigeria, Frederick instilled the centralized social system at the upper Niger and later the lower Niger basin. The ICG report on background to the conflict on Northern Nigeria suggests that Frederick's political system was based on his military warfare experience with the Fulanis. The "Fulani war-making race invokes, deploys, and reaps the benefits of war in extending their empire" (Ejiogu, 2013, p. 658). In Frederick's 1902 Annual Report to the British Colony he suggests that:

It is unfortunately true that the African savage in his primitive state can, as a rule, understand nothing but force, and regards arguments and verbal lesson as weapons of weak, to be listened to for the moment and set aside when convenient. (Ejiogu, 2013, p. 659)

Frederick installed Fulani rulers in each region he overtook. He reinstated the French deposed Bornu sheik and "secured alliance without bloodshed in the first major penetration of Lugard's regime" (Ejiogu, 2013, p. 659). Although "he denounced the Fulanis as alien and primitive," he continued to utilize their intelligence in attaining his goals, acknowledging them as "born rulers with wonderful intelligence as compared to the ability of the Negro tribes" (p. 659). Frederick succeeded in establishing Fulani rulers into his colonial regime and oppressed those who opposed the British presence such as the Satiru and Benue valley.

Frederick Lugard successfully co-opted the Fulani rulers and set autocratic social authority patterns as part of his colonial projects regime and a system of arbitrary rule in the upper Niger as a standing proof that he brought genius to the realm of colonial administration in Africa. (Ejiogu, 2013, p. 659)

The colonial administration continued to restructure other local authorities with their adopted political practice to create a complete local power base for furthering British interests. Local rulers were used to control the populace and raise revenue under the decision and supervision of British officials.

Although the colonial masters introduced significant political, judicial, and cultural changes, "they hardly disrupted the social structures of the regions including their dominant religion and culture" (Mustapha, 2004, p. 5). They constructed infrastructural developments which included railroads that ran from Lagos to the northern parts of the region to boost transportation of agricultural products from the North to other parts of the country. The construction of the railway lines between 1898 and 1912 created trading opportunities for the transportation of items between regions (p. 5). The railroads also provided trading opportunities and the migration of Southerners to Northern cities of Kano, Kaduna, and Zaria for better living conditions.

The International Crisis Group Working to Prevent Conflict Worldwide report suggests that although the migration resulted in the plurality of ethnic groups in the region, it "did not lead to greater ethnic integration in all cases" (ICG, 2010, p. 5). Strangers (indigenous migrants) were given different residential territories called Sabon-garis or strangers quarters by the autocratic Caliphates. British authorities stated the purpose for the policy was to preserve the North's Islamic identity. The ICG (2010) reports that the British discouraged the movement of non-Muslims into the core Muslim regions known as Sabon-garis to avoid intergroup conflicts (p. 5). Over time the distinction between locals (indigenes) and strangers emerged as key feature of Nigerian social and political life (p. 5). The separation increased ethno-religious identities and reinforced discriminatory practices between the Hausa-Fulani and other local dwellers (p. 5). Segregation of regions continued to prevail even at the secession of Hugh Clifford who tried to incorporate other regional local elites into the British colonial administration.

Colonial Regionalized Administration and Politicization

The British continued to run separate political and administration entities in the North and South outside of common economic infrastructures such as roads, railways, and common currency (Mustapha, 2004). At the succession of Lugard, Hugh Clifford tried to incorporate western-educated local elites into his administration as the governor between 1919 and 1925 (Mustapha, 2004, p. 4). He suggested to the "colonial office in London that the Nigerian state was a make-up of European theory that does not fit wholly into the environment of the people that arrive wholly from different stage of civilization" (p. 4). Clifford's 1922 Constitution proposed the integration of the two Southern Provinces and the Colony of Lagos with government participation for the Western-educated elites. A legislative council was established to replace the Northern Council and the Lagos Legislative Council with elections extended to local candidates outside of the colony.

In 1938 the National Youth Movement representing the new, educated elite superseded the Nigerian National Democratic Party (Mustapha, 2004, p. 5). Mustapha suggests that though both parties had national in their names; they were, however, a representation of the Lagos elites and its surrounding (p. 5). The National Council of Nigeria was formed in 1944 to drive better educational provisions for the locals. However, other Southern and Eastern minorities and a few people from the North were incorporated into the programs. Its implementation was, however, challenged by the post-world pressure and the states were quickly regionalized in its response. The 1946 Richards Constitution regionalization in response to the pressure corresponded to ethnicity with Hausa-Fulani in the North, Igbo in the East, and Yoruba in the South (p. 5). However, not only were the entire administration and fiscal structures of government finally regionalized, "Nigeria was also divided into movements for modern nationalism and westernized elites" (p. 5). The Western elites in the South represented the modernist nationalism while the more traditional nationalism in the North was based on the Islamic traditionalism and aristocratic symbolism. This action demonstrated that little was done to unify the institutions or integrate the people. Nigeria was described as "an internal geography of colonialism expression that emphasized the distinctiveness of the people and indissoluble connection" (p. 5). Each region was connected by their territories, tribesmen, and chiefs or elders.

The structural divide and rule "woven into the colonial state permeated the society and remains engrained in Nigerian Political life" (Mustapha, 2004, p. 7). By 1951 national political parties were firmly split along ethno-regional lines with the Hausa-Fulani dominating the National People's Congress (NPC) in the North. The

14

Yoruba dominated the Action Group (AG) in the West while the Igbos dominated the NCNC in the East. Each political party head was a representation of each region: Sir Ahmadu Bello for the Hausa-Fulani North, Dr. Nnamdi Azikiwe for the Igbos of the East, and Chief Obafemi Awolowo for the Yoruba West. They competed amongst themselves to succeed the departing colonial authorities and clashed over number of issues.

The years preceding independence "witnessed major instances of inter-ethnic violence" that included the Hausa and Igbo migrants clash in Kano in 1953 over attempts by Southern parties to hold anti-colonial and pre-independence rallies (ICG, 2010, p. 6). The clash "left over 21 Igbo men dead, 36 wounded and about 200 others injured" (p. 6). The ICG report suggests the violence reflected the opposition to independence of Northern politicians who feared that the end of the British rule would mean domination of the North by the more developed South (p. 6). Ejiogu (2013) also states that the clashes "demonstrated local resentment of Igbo economic domination especially in petty commerce" (p. 7). However, other religious oppositions and conflict included the Mahdism (a Muslim based anti-colonial movement) that "intended to strengthen Islam and triumph justice" in the British ruling system and continued to occur (ICG, 2010, p. 6). Their intensions of drawing the Northern indigenous ruling class and the British administration closer to avoid threat of losing the country's governance were misunderstood by the British. The ruling Sokoto Qadiriyya and Tijaniyya brotherhood tension increased as they accused its members of appropriating power and wealth and incorporating Western influence. The growing tension between the Islamic scholarly and political elites resulted to the numerous clashes in mid-1950s (ICG, 2010, p. 65). The height of the continued ethnical clash was the thirty month Biafran War that left millions including women and children dead.

1966/1967 coups and Biafran War. Although the 1967 Biafran War was tagged as a civilian war, most scholars suggest the war was inter-ethnical between the federal government dominated Hausa group and the secession Igbo Eastern group (Atofarati, 1992; Ejiogu, 2013; Njoku, 2013; Shibru, 2009). While the Northerners feared loss of power and favor, the Easterners complained of prolonged discrimination and inequality in distribution of power and resources.

Several reports suggest the 1966 coup preceding the recoup was carried out by Christian Igbo military officers against perceived religious and political dominations of the Northern NPC (Atofarati, 1992, para. 22; ICG, 2010, p. 8). Most Northern Nigerian political and religious leaders such as Ahmadu Bello (the then Prime Minister) were killed with the hope of shattering the Northern plan of "forging ahead with greater northern unity and restoring the heritage Caliphate" (ICG, 2010, p. 8). Virtually six months after the coup, a retaliation recoup by the Northerners was witnessed in July 1967.

The recoup was led this time by Colonel Yakubu Gowon—a Christian minority soldier from the middle belt, then under the Northern region (ICG, 2010, p. 8). Gowon was believed to be part of a compromise by Muslim leaders to retain the solidarity of the non-Muslim minorities in the Northern region (p. 8). Thousands of Southerners, mostly Igbo military men and civilians were killed, forcing them to flee to their region for safety and regroup for war.

The enthroned Head of State, Lt. Col. Yakubu Gowon, in a broadcast to the Northerners stated that he had received reports that Easterners living in the North were still being killed continually after the end of the coup (Atofarati, 1992). He pointed out that such actions were "beyond reasoning to the point of recklessness and irresponsibility" (Atofarati, 1992, para. 23). An ad hoc conference of representatives from all regions was called in Lagos to that effect. Legislation was drafted to help nullify extremes of centralization and posting of military personnel to lessen the tension. However, all Eastern military troops were deployed back to Enugu, their regional capital, while others were sent to Lagos or Kaduna (para. 28). The isolation of soldiers from the Eastern region was viewed as a gang-up by the federal government and other regions. Lt. Col Ojukwu (the Eastern Regional leader) "saw the action as signifying a mark of division between the Easterners and the rest of the nation" (para. 28). The Easterners began to prepare for secession following the deployment of their military personnel and flood of civilians back to their region.

At a peace negotiation between the Supreme Council of Federal Republic and Military Governors of Eastern Region at Aburi, Ghana, Ojukwu suggested that "to stay together, the regions must first draw apart" (Atofaratii, 1992, para 29). Ojukwu was suggested to have insinuated secession that prompted his rejection of the Aburi decree 8

16

formed with the aim of reuniting the regions (para. 30). Ojuwku rejected the degree stating it fell short of full implementation of the Aburi discussions and declared the Eastern region an independent state.

The major cause of the coups and succeeding war was in protest over the 1914 amalgamation of the three major regions (Ejiogu, 2013; Njoku, 2013; Shibru, 2009). Chinua Achebe suggests the violence was caused by European powers that "cobbled together several distinct nationalities that were naturally demarcated in sub regions into ill-fated Nigeria project like a piece of birthday chocolate cake" (Ejiogu, 2013, p. 654). Ojukwu also states the declaration of Biafra was an "act of liberation from death, insecurity and ethnic hegemony" while Ejike concluded that it was "the conclusion of a bitter political muscle-flexing between the federal government and the Eastern Nigerian government" (Ejiogu, 2013, p. 654). Ojukwu later surrendered to the Federal Government of Nigeria in January, 1970, and the war was declared as no victor, no vanquished with the Easterners reabsorbed back into the federation.

Summary

This chapter examined the geographical and political history of the major regions of Nigeria. British structuring of over 250 ethnic groups with different cultural, political, and religious values ignited struggles for power domination amongst the regions. Colonial divide-and-rule system, regionalization of administration, and politicization created fear and hatred amongst the regions. Violence in different parts of Nigeria especially in the major cities of Northern Nigeria continued to prevail even after the 1960 Independence as local elites struggled over political and economic advantage. Protests and violence continued to spring up with its heights as the 1967/1967 coups and Biafran War. Although the war ended with no victors, violence continues to be a recurring event in major Nigerian cities especially in major cities of Northern Nigeria. Human Identity theory that has been used in analyzing inter-ethnic violence arising due to governmental discrimination and inequality in political and economic power was applied.

Chapter 3

Human Identity Theories – relation to ethnicity and religion

Literature on the primordalism approach, instrumentalism, and constructivism has been used to analyze the conflict associated with economic and government factored violence that contribute to inter-ethnical conflicts (Bačová, 1998). Inter-ethnical conflict was mostly common with third world countries that went through British colonial administrative (Wimmer, 1997, p. 673). A majority of African and other heterogeneous countries that inherited colonial bureaucracies structured along ethnic lines were more likely to experience inter-ethnic conflict.

Nigeria is categorized as one of the most heterogeneous societies in the world (Wimmer, 1997, p. 637). Nigerian's ethnic characteristics and population are assumed to comprise about "400 different ethnic groups with over 250 languages" (Adeoti & Olaniyan, 2014, p. 105), while Okpanachi (2012) suggests there are "374 ethnic groups in Nigeria" (p. 5). Although there are three major recognized ethnic groups with Hausas in the North, Igbos in the East, and Yorubas in the South, there are other minor ethnic groups within the regions with multiple dialects and cultures. What the colonial masters merged as a Nigerian state is "a large territory that comprises of three major nations and several smaller ones" (Shibru, 2009, p. 18). The three major nations were "composed of three powerful constituent regions--the Northern, the (south-) Easter, and the (south-) Western--each with its own capital, its own parliament, cabinet, and high court, and its own budget" (Geertz, 1963, Part III, "Nigeria" sect., para. 2). The regions were dominated by major ethnic groups that comprised the Fulani/Hausa in the North, Yoruba in the South, and Igbo speaking groups in the East. The historical background of the country indicates that most of the ethnic groups were carved from the Niger basin with different geographical, religious, and cultural affiliations (Ejiogu, 2013). These ethnic groups were, however, merged into one country through the colonial 1914 Amalgamation decree irrespective of despairing characteristics.

Ethnic group is defined as "communities that share common connections in origin, decent, or kinship" that distinguish them from other groups (Bacik, 2002, p. 28). The groups share assumed biological, ancestral, and cultural connection that is unique to them. Ethnicity is, therefore, characterized by "common origins, history, culture, language and values" (Brown & Langer, 2010, p. 3). The ethnic identity of a group could range from language, dress, customs, values, and belief system (Irobi, 2005). Irobi suggests conflicts between ethnic groups could arise based on "race, religion, language or identity" (2005, p. 2). Ethnic conflict can be confused with other types of conflict due to different characteristics that define the concept.

However, ethnic conflict occurs "between ethnic groups within a multi-ethnic state" (Ismayilov, 2000, p. 53). While ethnic violence is assumed to occur between "different ethnic groups with different ethnic identities, inter-ethnic conflicts occur between different ethnic groups within a state" (Zeleke & Abate, 2005, p. 1). Kaufman (n.d.) suggests the connection of "religion and ethnicity is closely associated with linguistic identity as religion means more to the people than their geographical associations" (p. 8). Religion is believed to form people's identity and values as much as ethnicity does. People with the same norms and values intend to unite with their groups but are likely to pull away from others that differ from them.

Inter-ethnical conflicts could also arise due to "the ethnicisation of state bureaucracy" that divides groups and politicizes ethnic differences (Wimmer, 1997, p. 637). In Nigeria, the British colonial divide-and-rule system isolated ethnic groups from each other to prevent them from revolting against them. Its regionalized political system was transferred to local administration causing the groups to struggle against each other in domination of power and resources. Wimmer (1997) suggests ethnicity can be "used by political elites in state-building processes, but it can however become quickly politicized" (p. 631). The British administration in Nigeria manipulated the political system mostly for the imperial economic gains and its officials' security. Colonial sectional administration hindered the regions from fighting against the system and influenced struggle for domination of political power by the regions.

To better understand the concept of ethnicity, Bacik (2002) suggests a study of National Identity Theory. Ethnic nationalism defines national grouping by "physical characteristic, culture, religion, language, and common ancestry" (Bacik, 2002, p. 20). Bonding characteristics are assumed to encourage ethnic groups to naturally compete with others outside of their group for the purposes of retaining the benefits gained from their group. They are also assumed to discriminate against others for fear of losing such benefits.

Bacik (2002) suggests most inter-state conflicts are based on human identity—the mobilization of people in a community that share common race, religion, culture, and language. Ethnic conflict is categorized as identity conflicts that are part of internal conflicts of a state (Ismayilov, 2000, p. 514). The conflicts are assumed to revolve around identity and security issues where power contention exists. Dominant aspects of "ethnic conflicts are self-identification like name, religion or linguistic differences that are of historical importance to their identity" (Ismayilov, 2000, p. 52). Ethnic conflict is more likely to exist in a mixed community within a weak state, nation, or international authority (p. 59). Factors fueling such conflicts can be related to fear of losing resources to others, as well as imbalance and inequality in distribution and allocation of resources.

Ethnic conflicts occur due to unequal distribution of resources in a nation-state (Wimmer, 2000). Psychological fear of losing favors from colonialized administration and lack of knowledge in transitional governance can be a contributing factor in inter-ethnic conflict (Olu-Adeyemi, 2006). An example is the violence of the Africana group from South Africa on the democratic election night. However, ethnically diverse societies are known to experience different degrees of conflicts that range from a group's interest, fear of losing past favors, and struggles towards dominance of political and economic powers. Conflicts in Nigeria began to occur as far back as 1915 within the Kontagora, Kano, Bauchi, and Muri of the

21

upper Niger over imperialist favoring of the Fulani ruling classes (Ejiogu, 2013, p. 666). Segregation of ethnic groups and inclusion of others in bureaucratic decision instruments are believed to influence ethnic conflicts.

Inter-ethnic conflict can result in ethnic separation or secession (Pantazopolous, 1995). Ethnic separation entails ethnic groups demanding release from the legal ties of the state's constitutional arrangement (Ismavilov, 2000, p. 56). Ethnic war, however, occurs where secession and independence from the state might be demanded. The first recorded Nigerian inter-ethnical conflict was the 1967 Biafran War that emanated from the 1966 military coup. The Eastern Igbo-dominated region sort secession from the Nigerian-Hausa-dominated federal government due to marginalization in political powers and inequality in distribution of resources and infrastructures.

The colonial administration adopted the Fulani/Hausa political system and its institutions, co-opted its political elders in their administration, and favored them more in distribution of infrastructures such as railways and other basic amenities. While the North had ruled the country for about 36 years since it assumed independence in 1960, other south-south and south-west regions ruled for 12 years while the south-east only ruled for six months (Onyeani, 2014). Within the 53 years of Nigeria's independence, the North continues to dominate the federal governance.

The cause of the war was attributed by many scholars to the amalgamation of the three major distinct regions as a state by the colonial administration (Irobi, 2005; Mustapha, 2004; Olu-Adeyemi, 2006). The Biafran War, popularly known as the Nigeria Civil War, was fought by the Eastern region of Nigeria against the Northern-dominated federal government. The Eastern region declared itself an independent state which was regarded as an act of rebellion by the federal military government of Nigeria (Atofarati, 1992). Secession or separatism is a "demand for formal withdrawal from a central political authority by a member of a unit based on the claim for independent" sovereignty (Pantazopolous, 1995, p. 1). Units demanding for secession want to be legitimized to rule their own land as a separate entity.

Other issues of ethnic conflicts include "recognition and protection of minority interest within a society" (Ismayilov, 2000, p. 54). Chinua Achebe's book entitled *There was a Country: A Personal History of Biafra* "advances the argument of humanistic and democratic principles and the need for re-exploring African risks and political systems in the positive" (Mudimbe, 2013, p. 675). The inability of international bodies to interfere or investigate the massive killings of the Igbo ethnic group by the Northern dominated federal government of Nigeria as in other genocides was seen as international injustice (Njoku, 2013). Achebe suggests that there has been "no real closure to the political defeat" as the war was declared no victor, no vanquished and question of whether an actual Nigerian state exists still lingers (as cited in Mudimbe, 2013, p. 676). Biafran War secession groups were reabsorbed into the federation and were labeled as rebels. Reinforcing national unity and marginalizing ethnical representation in institutional bureaucratic arrangements encourages inequality that ignites ethnic violence (Brown & Langer, 2010). The fear of them rebelling in the near future is always present.

Harris and Reilly (1998) suggest that proper analysis of inter-ethnic conflict will entail "identifying the history, core issues, and participants of the conflicts" (p. 348). Education of transitional strategies, creating awareness on the existence of ethnic tension, and strengthening of the economic base can help reduce inter-ethnic conflicts (Zeleke & Abate, 2005). Involving or implementing external programs as one-solution-fits-all should be avoided for lasting strategies.

Three themes of Primordalism, Instrumentalism, and Constructivism of the human identity theory have been applied by many scholars in analyzing inter-ethnic conflicts (Bačová, 1998; Blagojevic, 2009; Brown & Langer, 2010; Geertz, 1963). While the primordalism approach assumes the connection of ethnic identity as natural and biological, instrumentalism suggests ethnic affiliation is by choice and is, therefore, flexible. Individuals can choose what social group to belong to for economic and other beneficial gains. Constructivists, however, "believe that social systems give rise to conflicts along ethnic lines" (Tong, 2009, p. 63). Connections to such conflicts are assumed to be as a result of historical processes such as colonial manipulations. British colonial relations of most African countries and political elite manipulations for economic and power gains are associated with the theory.

Primordialism. Geertz' primordialism theory listed connections of ethnic groups as religion, language, and custom, in addition to its blood affiliation (Geertz, 1963). Relationships under this theory are for common interest or obligation rather than personal affiliation. Although relationship attachment is rooted in inherited ties such as culture or kin connection, beyond these ties are "being born into a particular religious community, speaking a particular language,...and following particular social practices" (Geertz, 1963, Part II, para. 1). An individual's level of attachment to these ties can be influenced by the importance they or societies place on them.

Weir (2012) argued that primordialism could not be applied to the case of the Rwandan genocide, suggesting that the Hutu and Tutsi tribes were found to have similar characteristics such as language, traditions, and taboos (p. 1). The historical origin of the ethnic groups could not be traced. The cause of ethnic conflict was attributed to political leaders' struggles over economic needs, greed, and grievances (p. 1). Ethnic conflict was manipulated for political and economic gains.

In developed or modernized countries primordial ties could be expressed through political parties. Geertz (1963) suggests primordial ties by race, language, and religion can be stronger in modern societies where the state is weak and need for effective welfare for the poor is misunderstood (Part II, para. 2). Therefore, race ties could be visible in a multicultural society such as the United States where political competition is high and racial discriminations between the white and black races are visible.

Oganesyan (2009) analyzed the Caucasus violent conflicts and wars that led to the massacre and displacement of populations such as the Soviet Union (p. 2). Despairing ethnic characteristics such as cultural traditions, languages, and religion were visible and were attributed to contributing to the "Nagorno-Karabakh conflict of 1988 and the Armenia/Azerbaijan war of 1992/1994" (p. 3). The conflict between the groups continues to recur.

Unitary states are also assumed to be more stable than multilingual because people under the former assume binding common ties that override the conflicts arising from economic or social issues. The common oneness of a unitary state makes those "who are charged with it feel that they are kith and kin" (Geertz, 1963, Part II, para. 3). Existence of multilingual language in a state is assumed to generate suspicion that influences conflict. Primordial ties, however, were found prominent with groups who are not of the same kind due to oppositions in belonging to another group.

In modern societies, however, struggles in not belonging to other groups are assumed to help form the basis for a democratic and stable state. Distancing one's self from belonging to another group can be understood as "tribalism, parochialism, communalism, and so on... [with regard to]...the problems faced by new states" (Geertz, 1963, Part II, para. 4). Other competing loyalties of a new state could be "class ties, party, business, professional or other self-standing ties" (para. 15). These ties associate themselves with a political system they trust. While economic associated ties are believed to encourage revolution, dissatisfaction based on race, language, or culture threatens a partition or merger.

In the case of Nigeria, existing ethnic groups carved from different geographical, political, and religious backgrounds continue to clash. Their glaring distinguished language, culture, norms, and values are highly prominent. Each ethnic group assumes strong kinship relations as blood ties. Merging of 250 ethnic groups with about 400 languages in Nigeria was against the British instituted constitution of what would be called a nation as "a body that has the same traditions, language, and institutions" (Mudimbe, 2013, p. 673). Although "existence of cultural differences is not the primary cause of conflict," cross-cultural conflict occurs between individuals separated by cultural boundaries (Avruch, 1998, p. 5). In applying the influence of primordial attachment to the issue of a merger, Geertz (1963) states that the Nigerian issue was one of the most dramatic, complex, unbelievable, and extreme situations (Part III, "Nigeria" sect., para. 6). Geertz categorized the primordial loyalties and antipathies with a primordial group surrounding the tension in the Nigerian state as the strongest in the world's history (para. 6). In recounting the agony of the coups and Biafran War, Geertz (1963) suggests that in Nigeria:

political institutions [were] hurriedly put together in the last hectic years constitution-making before independence, lacking a comprehensive national party, a supereminent political leader, an overarching religious tradition or a common cultural background. (Part III, "Nigeria" sect., para. 7)

Their local elites were described as individuals with several minds that did not know what to do with the freedom they received. However, the causes of the coup were not only blamed on primordial ties. "[T]he involvement of great powers...complex and intense and narrowly balanced pattern of group distrust" (Geertz, 1963, Part III, "Nigeria" sect., para. 9) were suggested as contributing factors as well.

Instrumentalism. Instrumentalism, however, views ethnic affiliations in "social, political, and economic competitions" (Brown & Langer, 2010, p. 4). Instrumentalism views ethnicity as a resource for political elites to define and regulate group memberships. Ethnic elites sometimes use ethnic differences to influence "hostility from inequality and power disparity within their communities to the elites of other communities" (p. 5). While instrumentalism recognizes blood ties, it places importance to relationships of other kinds. This kind of relationship is "based on national awareness, not closeness but the need for protection of common interest" (Bacova, 1998, p. 33). They could be likened to the ones prevalent in "trade unions, political parties, sports club or other interest groups" (p. 33). Individuals are assumed to choose a particular ethnic identity by weighing the economic costs and benefits of such groups. Therefore, ethnic attachment is "for the protection of common interest," and community is the instrument for achievement of goals (Bacova, 1998, p. 33). Ethnic identity is, therefore, by choice rather than fixed or inherited. This means individuals can identify with societies of their choice based on economic or political benefits (Bacova, 1998; Tong, 2009). Ethnicity can, therefore, become competitive and ties can be used for the furthering of one's goals.

Increased regional conflicts in Nigeria can be attributed to colonial manipulation of regions that transitioned to the creation of political parties along ethnic lines. Each region represented by their political elites struggled to ascend to the highest level of government for economic and power competitions. The height of the struggles became visible in emerged coups, recoups, and finally, to the quest for secession that led to the Biafran War in which millions of lives were lost. Chinua Achebe alleged the coups and war were calculated attempts towards the elimination of the Igbo ethnic group from the state (Njoku, 2013, p. 711). Geertz (1963) suggests the war was like waiting for a prophecy to unfold.

In January 1966 a military coup led to the death of a number of Northern political leaders, including Sir Abubakar Tafawa Balewa, and the establishment of Ibo-led military regime. A second coup, led by a Northerner...Colonel Yakubu Gowon, eventuated in the massacre of somewhere between ten to thirty thousand Ibos living in Hausa areas of North, while anywhere from two hundred thousand to a million and a half Ibos fled from the North to their Eastern region homeland. In May of 1967, Colonel Gowon assumed emergency powers and sought to divide the Eastern region into three states as a device to increase the power of the non-Ibo Easterners and decrease that of the Ibos. The Ibos, forming themselves into the Republic of Biafra, rebelled, and, after nearly three years of some of the most bitter warfare of modern times...more than two million people were killed. (Part IV, "Nigeria" sect., para. 8)

The war was assumed to be more of regional power struggles between the North and the East.

Tong (2009) suggests ethnic violence under instrumentalism is usually interest-based factored by the manipulation of elites (p. 65). "Ethnic identities become seriously amenable to political manipulation either when suppressed groups feel marginalized from political and economic processes affecting them" (p. 65). While Ojukwu suggested the succession was intended to liberate the country from the division it was experiencing, Gowon felt there was a need in keeping the regions as a state.

Instrumentalism has been applied to most African ethnic conflicts such as Cote d'Ivoire, Ghana, Kenya, and Tanzania (Tong, 2009). Colonial structuring of most African countries with different ethnic characteristics and politicization along ethnic groups influenced instrumentalism theory. The reason why certain democratic institutions experience violence and others do not is attributed to the lack of political institutions such as freedom of press and proper procedures of government. It becomes difficult to decide whether or not strong democratic institutions encourage civic engagement (Weir, 2012, para. 5). However, in most African nations, ethnic

27

unrest was found to be the major reason for violence rather than availability of institutions.

Constructivism. Constructivism is "manufactured rather than given and emerges when a social group interacts with another social group" (Shibru, 2009, p. 18). Its significance on the group's identity varies because of its constructed nature (p. 18). Therefore, it places more emphasis on the structures of societal institutions in ensuring ethnic peace. The major explanation of constructivism is that ethnicity is made rather than inherited. With regard to societies that experienced colonialism, constructivism argues that "ethnic cleavages are a creation of colonial power through immense power of colonial masters and its "divisions have endured and will last for a long time" (p. 18). The 1994 Hutu-Tutsi massacre was related to the outcome of the reconstruction of ethnicity by Belgians that categorized the country and later shaped it into two religious groups over time (p. 19). These identities transformed the people and played a major role in the Rwanda 1994 genocide war.

Three elements emphasized in transforming identities through constructivism theories include historical account of the people for comprehensive understanding of their politicization of ethnicity, the distinctiveness and wide elastic nature of ethnicity, and its wide variety of potential ethnic groups (Shibru, 2009, p. 18). These elements are eminent in Nigeria due to its vast experience with British colonialization. Colonialism has been significant in Nigeria's identity, political processes, and religion. Colonial masters influenced and nurtured the creation of an 'us' versus 'them' syndrome: Muslim versus Christian; Northern versus Southerner; Hausa-Fulani versus Yoruba versus Igbo; and so on (Okpanachi, 2012, p. 4). British colonial governance structured and maintained the Northern and Southern regional administration for the imperialist's security and economic benefits even after the 1914 amalgamation degree. Geertz (1963) described the Nigerian political arrangement as "a federal one, composed of three powerful constituent regions" (Part III, "Nigeria" sect., para. 1)—the Northern (Fulani-Hausa), the Eastern (Igbo), and the Southern (Yoruba). Politics became a struggle over regional dominance through their political representative.

The ICG (2010) states that the impact of regionalism and localism through the divide-and-rule system in education, economic, and political "created imbalances that later became significant in the mobilization and manipulation in identity consciousness and competitive politics" (p. 5). While the Easterners and Southerners were favored with educational abilities, the Northerner's political system was adopted with its representatives and extended to other regions.

Colonial influence in the political and economic life of Nigeria has evolved since World War II. Political parties are regionalized with political parties dominated by a particular ethnic group. The Hausa, Ibo, and Yoruba as the major regions and the Northern People's Congress (NPC), the National Council of Nigeria and the Cameroons (NCNC), and the Action Group (AG) for the regions respectively (Geertz, 1963, Part III, para. 2). Each political party was designated with local political elite, and they competed against each other over dominance of federal power and resources, taking attention away from the foreign rulers.

Liberation and institution of democratic tools are assumed to help minimize ethnic conflicts. This assumption is based on the idea that political liberation encourages violence while violence decreases with the institution of democracy. Liberation was defined as the loosening of political control such as freedom of press, and institutionalization of proper procedure of government that eliminates illegal arrests and torture of people (Tong, 2009). Democratic institutions, therefore, provide avenues for individuals and groups to express themselves without resorting to violence. Violence is lessened when citizens believe that the state can address their issues or that media can help voice out their concerns (Tong, 2009, p. 61). Free press becomes essential in the institutionalized approach.

Lack of proper democratic institutions has been attributed to the rise of ethnic violence in most developing countries like Nigeria. Tong suggests Kenya Daniel Arap Moi used military coup to ignite ethnic conflicts (2009, p. 72). Although Sub-Saharan Africa is significant for primordialist and instrumentalism theories because of ethnic tensions and lack of resources, instrumentalism, however, was found to be more applicable. Political manipulation of colonial divide-and-rule systems, military coups, and rigging of elections synonymous with the Nigerian system can be associated with constructivism theory. Lack of institution of proper procedures could be deliberate or based on ignorance of the requirements of democratic institutions.

In conceptualizing the relationship between religion and conflict in identity theories, Stein (2011) suggests "religious differences lead to conflict due to the central role it plays in constituting individual and group identity" (para. 8). The importance individuals or society attaches to religion as part of their ethnic identity affects how religion can influence conflict. Where such attachment is strong, political leaders can use religion as the basis for inciting violence and justifying their aims. Huntington's theory that "civilizations are differentiated by history, language, and culture is used in strengthening how individual and society's views about religion impact conflict" (Stein, 2011, p. 22). How people interpret religion and what a relationship with God should be were found as contributing factors.

Stein (2011) states these differences have "generated prolonged and the most violent conflicts" than other cultural meaning in historical times (p. 22). Religion offers response to the human need in developing "a secure identity and sense of locatedness" (p. 7). Religion is a major distinctive factor between the North and South in Nigeria. Ethnical cultures such as mode of dressing, food, language, and accompanying norms and values are shaped by religious affiliations of the regions. It becomes difficult to separate Northern Nigerian culture and their Muslim religious demands as in most Muslim affiliated societies like Lebanon and other Arabic countries.

Religion generally forms individual's worldviews and can be used as a "continuous means to maintain the psychological stability individuals need" (Stein, 2011, p. 22). Following the importance of religion in forming individuals' identity, the presence of other religious groups can threaten the identity since "religion often inspires believers to abide by customs and behavior rules that increase the visibility of inter-group differences" (p. 22). For example, non-Muslims in Nigeria or other societies are referred to as infidels; their presence is seen as a corruption of the values individuals share. Christians, on the other hand, view others as sinners and outcasts that cannot inherit the kingdom of God.

Instrumentalists recognize religion to play a vital role in conflict. Religion becomes a tool used by self-interested elites to mobilize support for fighting power in conflicts (Stein, 2011, p. 23). Political elites seeking power can use religion as an agent to manipulate the masses in pursuing economic and political ambitions to improve strategic advantage (p. 23). "Instrumentalist draws on collective organization and unifying mission or identity to motivate masses to kill and be killed" (p. 23). Religion is used as a reason to take up arms and self-sacrifices. Stein sites "how Serbian nationalists propaganda in Bosnian war portrayed Muslim Slavs as 'Christ-killers'" (p. 23). Nigerian leaders have continually used religion as a tool in an attempt towards extending their scope of power and territories. About 3,000 people were killed in Kaduna over the introduction of Sharia in twelve states in a purported attempt to declare Nigeria a Muslim state (Sampson, 2012, p. 107). Using religion as a worldview for conflicts draws in other believing groups outside of the territories to reinforce the conflict. In 1982, riots broken out in Kano and Kaduna over the United States' invasion of Afghanistan (p. 112). In response to the April, 2014, kidnapping of about 234 girls from the Government Secondary School in Chibok by Boko Haram, Onyeani suggests the action is a conspiracy from the North to take powers from the current Nigerian President Goodluck Jonathan from the Eastern region (Onyeani, 2014). However, others have accused the president of refusing to take action because the kidnapped girls are not from the Eastern region of his origin.

In summary, the constructivism perspective can help "shape actors' identities which in turn shape conflict behavior, it can also be interpreted as helping diffuse violence or encouraging peace and unity" (p. 24). Stein concludes that whether religious violence prevails depends on the interpretation given to it by individuals and societies. Constructivism and the instrumentalist perspectives in religious conflict of ethnicity are overlapping.

Summary

While primordialism, instrumentalism, and constructivism are applied in explaining ethnic conflicts, they are also used to analyze ethnic conflicts occurring within religious lines. Primordalism explains such conflicts can be due to association under assumed blood ties or kinship that is inherited. Instrumentalism suggests societal ties are through institutions and relations with societies based on economic or other self-interests. Individuals have the right to change their ties based on their level of benefit. Instrumentalists suggest people can change these ties in the same way they can choose to assume ties with societies, whether they speak their languages or not. Constructivism, however, blames ethnic violence on the structures of institutions in societies. Democratic structures such as free speech and media that enable people to voice their views are assumed to help lessen ethnic conflict.

Since religion is a major part of individual identity, political elites can use religion as an instrument to justify their political and economic aims. The masses can be mobilized into use of arms and deadly weapons for self-interests. Institutional and group support can be generated under this category for power gains. However, individuals' or societies' ties to these themes depend on the importance attached to them.

Chapter 3

Data Collection

Qualitative holistic single-case design was applied for this study to examine the role of inter-ethnic influence in the Northern Nigeria religious violence. A case study involves the study of an issue explored through one or more cases within a particular setting or context (Yin, 1989). As a method of research in qualitative studies, single-case study can be used "where the test represents a critical test of existing theory, where the case is a rare or unique event, or where the case serves to a revelatory purpose" (Yin, 1989, p. 45). Multiple data collection can be attained through observation, interviews, audiovisuals, documents, and reports (Yin, 1989, p. 73; see also Willis, 2007). Both the qualitative and case study approaches support the use of different sources for detailed understanding and description of the issue.

Multiple data collection procedures were used to justify conclusions based on similarities of information obtained (Willis, 2007, p. 219; Yin, 1989, p. 13). Multiple evidence flows from theoretical framework, histories, interviews, observations, and other forms of data collection.

Analytic generalization of case study "compares results of multiple experiments (or multiple surveys) to previously developed theory to obtain empirical results" (Yin, 1989, p. 13) of the study. Results obtained from the study are intended "to increase reader's understanding of phenomenon under study, bring about new discoveries or meanings, conform or extend what is already known" (Willis, 2007, p. 239). Inductive and deductive methods are applied to "work back and forth between practice and explanatory theory" in the data analysis process (Willis, 2007, p. 213). Analogical reasoning is usually used to seek partial similarities or understanding with results obtained.

Several features that qualified this study as a qualitative case study include:

- Identification of the case study as religious violence in Northern Nigeria and its influences as a case.
- Data collection for the study was "bounded" within a three-month-time period with multiple study of the cases from four major city settings of Kano, Jos, Kaduna, and Zaria where the violence occurs.
- Detailed description of the "history and chronological events" were examined through the pre-colonial geographical and political background, colonial regionalized administration and politicization, and the 1966/1967 coups and the Biafran War to uncover the contextual conditions surrounding the issue.
- Different data collection techniques were used through structured and non-structured interviews, historical data, and quantitative data. Oral interviews were conducted from participants that experienced violence in the cities of Kano, Jos, Kaduna, Jos, and Zaria based on reports of recurring violence from review of literature.
- Finally, interpretative generalization was attained by comparing data collected in the sites, in themes of sites, age groups, and historical data.

Acknowledging multiple perspectives recognizes that basic conditions of human existence impact human behavior (Willis, 2007, p. 191). These multiple perspectives mean that the study is subjective and seeks different methods to bring in-depth understanding of the study.

Case study is mostly preferred when the questions of "how" and "why" are posed and when the researcher has little control over the events (Yin, 1989, p. 13). These questioning methods limit the researcher's power over the participants and encourage focus on the phenomenon of study. The general framework of case study involves overlapping phases according to the need and issue of research that includes data collection, gaining entry and maintaining rapport, and data analysis and report.

Purposeful sampling in major conflict areas

Data collection starts with a proposal on how data would be collected, analyzed, and interpreted throughout the study (Willis, 2007, p. 198). Creswell (2007) and Yin (1989) suggest the first process is to identify the site or sites, programs, events, or individuals of study. Data collection through *purposeful sampling* in major sites of Northern Nigeria that include Kano, Kaduna, and Zaria with highly mixed religious and ethnic population where the religious violence is intense was used to seek different views of participants to the issue (Creswell, 2007, p. 37; Willis, 2007, p. 241). Data collection was made through "structured and non-structured interviews, historical data and qualitative data" (Willis, 2007, p. 241). Historical documents of federal cabinets, ministerial, and military school distribution according to regions from the independence period were collected mostly from government records and scholarly journals. The purpose was to find connection of political and economic struggles amongst the regions as suggested from the review of literature.

Questions with demographics that include participants' age, ethnic group, and experience of any of the violence were asked. A twenty to thirty minute interview was scheduled for each participant within their choice of venue.

Setting and Participant Selection Procedure

Selection of settings for this study was through the informative-oriented sampling method that is synonymous with case study research (Yin, 1989, p. 48). Selection of setting for research and participants was informed by information from the literature review. Qualitative researchers collect data in the field where participants experience the issue or problem under study (Creswell, 2007, p. 38). Information from review of literature documented that violence has been a recurring in the major cities of Jos, Kano, Zaria, and Kaduna before the 1960 independence and after the Biafran War. The 1966 coup that was assumed to have been carried out by the Eastern region military against the Northerners and the 1967 retaliating coup were intense within these locations. The outbreak of the 1967 Biafran War was preceded by intense killings of Igbo ethnic groups within these locations that prompted their massive exodus to their region to regroup for war. Subsequent violence has been occurring after the war in the major cities of Northern Nigeria.

Interviews

Most qualitative research studies involve framing questions and asking them to generate informative stories from participants (Willis, 2007, p. 246). "Interviews may be structured, semi-structured or open" (p. 245). I adopted semi-structured interviews that included demographics such as age, ethnic group, and experience of any religious conflicts. Only adults and those that witnessed any violence were selected for the interview.

I worked with different social, religious groups and individuals to help sort participants to the study. Letters were distributed to the leaders of the groups scheduling appointments to discuss the research study and ask for permission to be at their meetings to have one-on-one interviews with participants on the study. Based on the result of the response, face-to-face interviews were extended to twenty-eight participants that experienced violence in Northern Nigeria. The interviews lasted from twenty to thirty minutes per participant for proper narration of their experiences.

A flexible and friendly attitude was maintained, and the need for finding comprehensive result to the Northern Nigeria violence was emphasized to participants (Willis, 2007, p. 246). Participants were informed that their participation was voluntary and that either they or the researcher could withdraw from the process at any time. Confidentiality of the information provided was made known and documented in all letters issued.

Documents

Single-case studies can incorporate subunits of analyses for a more complex design development (Yin, 1989, p. 44). Multiple sources of data were obtained through documents, historical data, and quantitative data in addition to structured and unstructured interviews (Creswell, 2007, p. 73; Willis, 2007, p. 241; Yin, 1989, p. 37). Historical data of Federal Cabinet distribution in the following categories were compiled.

Composition of Federal Cabinet:

- List of Military Heads of States/Presidents by ethnic and regional groups from 1960 to 2014
- Ministers of the Abuja Federal Capital Territory from 1979 to 2014
- Supreme Court Chief Justices/Associate Justices from 1993
- Governors of Central Bank from 1960 independence to 2014
- Chiefs of the Nigerian Army from 1956 to 2014 by ethnic and regional groups
- Ministers of Defense from 1975 to 2014 by ethnic and regional groups
- Zonal composition of Nigerian Army Education School prior to 1967 war

A matrix of the records was compiled in ethnic and regional groups' categories and analyzed in pre- and post-independence eras to provide interpretation of regional power and resource struggles before the Biafran War and present based on theoretical frameworks knowledge (Creswell, 2007, p. 225; Willis, 2007, p. 241). The documents were compiled from reliable sources such as journals, newspapers, government records, and websites.

All access routes and decisions made throughout the research process as a "practical way of developing ethics checklist" and ensuring ethical and methodological considerations were adhered to (Creswell, 2007, p. 67). The oral interviews were recorded through audio recording device.

Other field notes such as journal jottings were "stored in a data collection matrix and information to protect the anonymity of participants" (Creswell, 2007, p. 142). In this study, names of participants were not needed in the interviews, and names of social groups of interviews were not identified. Records were separated according to sites (units), and age groups (49 and above, or 48 and under).

Other data storing mechanisms to secure information, as well as ensure anonymity and confidentiality of participants include:

- Backup copies of computer files for processed information
- Use of high-quality audio-recording device for interviews with proper fitting tape size
- Development of master list of types of information gathered
- Development of data collection matrix for proper location and identification of information (p. 143).

The documents will be stored for up to five years within which information could be used to extend research or publish, and later destroyed.

Reflective Journals

The reflective model assumes that most important problems in social sciences cannot be stated as well-formed issues and solved with performed solution (Willis, 2007, p. 204). Reflection in qualitative research allows researchers to organize, change, and formulate their perspectives, beliefs, and practices (p. 204). Reflecting is mostly done through journaling which researchers share with others such as their support or interest groups to let them understand their experiences in the process. Willis recommends that journaling in the form of a diary be kept while conducting qualitative research (p. 205). A reflective journal was kept about my feelings, assumptions, reactions, and experiences with participants. The diary was different from notes on data collected because it "helps researchers focus on issues that seem important" (p. 205). The diary mostly documented personal experiences and participants behaviors, for example those that restricted participation and those that accepted and why and other occurrences. Insights generated helped reduce reliance on pure data and increase the use of reasoning in the analysis process.

Data Analysis

Categorical aggregation was used to establish themes and patterns to attain naturalistic generalization (Creswell, 2007, p. 163). A data matrix of results of interviews and emanating documents was compiled in the following categories:

- Sites (Kano, Kaduna, Jos, and Zaria)
- Interviews (pre-post Biafran War of the 28 participants)
- Historical data of Federal Cabinet distribution (pre- and post-independence periods)

Thematic analysis of the interview results was made according to the four site units of the study; each unit was independently analyzed (Creswell, 2007, p. 75). Later, a cross-case analysis was used to compare results of each site against other sites. *Assertions or interpretative* meaning was drawn based on cross comparison results (p. 75). The efforts of interpretative research include categorical aggregation, description of the case, and established patterns, for possible generalizations as the conclusions (Creswell, 2007, p. 240; Willis, 2007, p. 163). Synthesis analytical technique was used to compare results of each group in one site of study against other groups in other sites (Creswell, 2007, p. 240). As earlier stated, the collected data from the four sites of study was categorized and coded according to the sites, and age brackets (48 and under and 48 and above) without indicating participants names.

The themes for interview and data analysis are:

a)   Kano, Kaduna, Jos, and Zaria;

c)   Age group (49 and above - pre-independence era, and 48 and under - post-independence era);

- Composition of Federal Cabinets; List of Military Heads of States/Presidents by ethnic and regional groups from 1960 to 2014
- Ministers of Defense from 1960 to 2014 by ethnic and regional groups
- Chiefs of the Nigerian Army from 1956 to 2014 by ethnic and regional groups
- Supreme Court Chief Justices/Associate Justices from 1993
- Governors of Central Bank from 1960 independence to 2014
- Zonal composition of Nigerian Army colleges and unit disposition prior to 1967 war

Direct interpretation was used to develop naturalistic generation based on the interviews and documents (Creswell, 2007, p. 157).

Data Representation

An in-depth picture of the case was presented through a narrative format of the tables and figures of interviews and documents; data were used to find connection to power and resources that influence inter-ethnic violence in line with the literature reviewed (Creswell, 2007, p. 157). These data were analyzed as I thought about and wrote them (Willis, 2007, p. 239). Additional data were not required to clarify the issue based on the volume of data collected.

The Case

Nigeria is known as one of the most heterogeneous countries in the world with over 400 ethnic groups and about 250 languages (Irobi, 2005; Okapnachi, 2012; Olu-Adeyemi, 2006). The British colonial administration merged these groups with diverse characteristics from the Upper and Lower Niger Basin to form what is known as the country of Nigeria today. Regionalized administration and politicization was adopted for the Northern and Southern regions even after the 1914 amalgamation.

Based on constructed railroads in the Northern region that linked other regions, most Southerners migrated to the North for business advantage. Conflict began to break out amongst the regions before 1914 to 1960 independence based protests over amalgamation, fear of loss of favor, and struggle over power dominance by the regions. Although the country has attained its independence, violence of different types has continued to spring up in different parts of the country, especially in the major cities of Northern Nigeria. Different scholars have analyzed the conflict as religious related between the dominant Muslim Hausa and non-indigenous Christian groups living in the region (Olu-Adeyemi, 2006, para. 10). Based on the analysis, different religious conflict resolution strategies by government, as well as non-profit and international agencies have been applied without major successful results.

The choices of Kano, Kaduna, Jos, and Zaria for this study were based on past history of recurring violence as reported by the

International Crisis Group Working to Prevent Conflict Worldwide, Society for Research and academic reports, and African Center for Strategic Research and Studies, Abuja.

Jos (capital of Plateau state in which Zaria is situated). In September 2001, about 1,000 people were killed after regular Friday Muslim prayers over what was termed as religious violence after Muslim prayers in Jos. In the same month of September 7-17, 2001, over 300 people were killed over an attack of a Christian woman who attempted to cross a public highway barricaded by Muslim worshippers. About 200 people were also killed over a disputed local government election in November, 2008. Sampson (2012) also reported that in January and March 2010 about 149 and 120 people were killed respectively in a two day violence spree between Christian and Muslim gangs in Jos (p. 107). In January 17-20, 2009, about 320 people were killed over resurgence of religious crisis, and over 500 women and children were killed by Fulani Muslims in Christian dominated villages within the Zaria Local Government in May 22, 2010.

Kano. In Kano, several post-independence violence episodes were reported throughout the major cities of Kano. Confrontation between Maitatsine (fundamentalist Muslim group) and police at a rally sparked massive week-long rioting, resulting in hundreds of deaths in 1980. In 1982, about 44 people were killed over assumed Muslim Students Society protest in the laying of an Anglican Church foundation stone by Archbishop Canterbury. In July 22, 1999, several casualties occurred "over reprisal to the Sagamu crisis of Ogun" (Sampson, 2012, p. 112). In the year 2000, Christian opposition to Sharia law lead to Christian-Muslim clashes in Kaduna and Kano leading to hundreds of deaths. In October 12, 2001, over 150 persons were killed in protest of the U.S. invasion of Afghanistan over Osama Bin Laden.

Kaduna. The *International Crisis Group Working to Prevent Conflict Worldwide* reported that an estimated 3,000 people died in riots over the introduction of Sharia law in February 21-22, 2000 (pp. 31-33). On November 16, 2002 over 250 people were killed and several churches were destroyed over the Miss World crisis (Sampson, 2012, pp. 107-112). These are just samples from inexhaustible lists of violence in the selected study sites to justify reasons for their selection.

Ethical Considerations

Satisfactory completion of the ethical approval form at the beginning of the study and obtaining approval was ongoing and renegotiated with the participants throughout the study process (Mauthner, Birch, Jessop, & Miller, 2002). Information about the study was provided to the participants, and the choice to opt-out of the process was made known. Gatekeepers to access participants were identified. Letters were written indicating the purpose of study and asking for their permission to interview the participants as voluntarily. Some such gatekeepers were clergies in charge of churches, groups, or other publicity personnel assigned for that purpose.

Access, Informed Consent, and Rapport

In qualitative research, decisions need to be made about who or what should be sampled, what form of sampling will take place, and how many people or sites need to be sampled (Willis, 2007, p. 125). Sampling for this study was based on the four major Northern Nigerian cities of Kano, Kaduna, Jos, and Zaria where violence is usually intense based on historical records of its mixed religious and ethnic population.

Proper protocol was adhered to by sending out letters that stated the intended purpose of the research to examine the influence of ethnicity in the religious violence. Individuals were interviewed at their selected choice of venue to protect their privacy. Other ethical provisions as listed in institutional review board (IRB) format such as participants' voluntary participation in the study, the ability to withdraw from the process at will, and risks associated with the study were properly disclosed before the interview processes began.

The study lasted for a collective period of ninety days (three months)—approximately thirty days for each site as bounded by time and space in case study format (Yin, 1989, p. 49). The purpose of subunits in single-case study according to Yin (1989) is to enable the researcher to "add significant opportunities for extensive analysis, enhancing the insights into the single case" (p. 44). The report of the study was based on comparison of the theory development, as well as the findings from data collection.

Consent forms stating that the participants and the researcher have the right to terminate the process at any time was provided and signed by all parties. Information about the process was provided to the pastors and participants. Consent was sought from all other officials and personnel in charge of decision making in the library, archives, and public places where records needed for the research were available in order to have access to the records during the period the research covered. Permission for the access was "negotiated prior to each interview" (Yin, 1989, p. 63). A clause on the consent forms indicating confidentiality of shared information was provided as well.

Overall, Creswell (2007) supports the entrance and data collection process of this study that answers the following questions:

a) Why the site was chosen for study

b) What will be done at the site during the research and for how long

c) Will the researcher's presence be disruptive

d) How will study be reported

e) What will the gatekeeper, participants, and site gain from the study? (p. 128)

f)

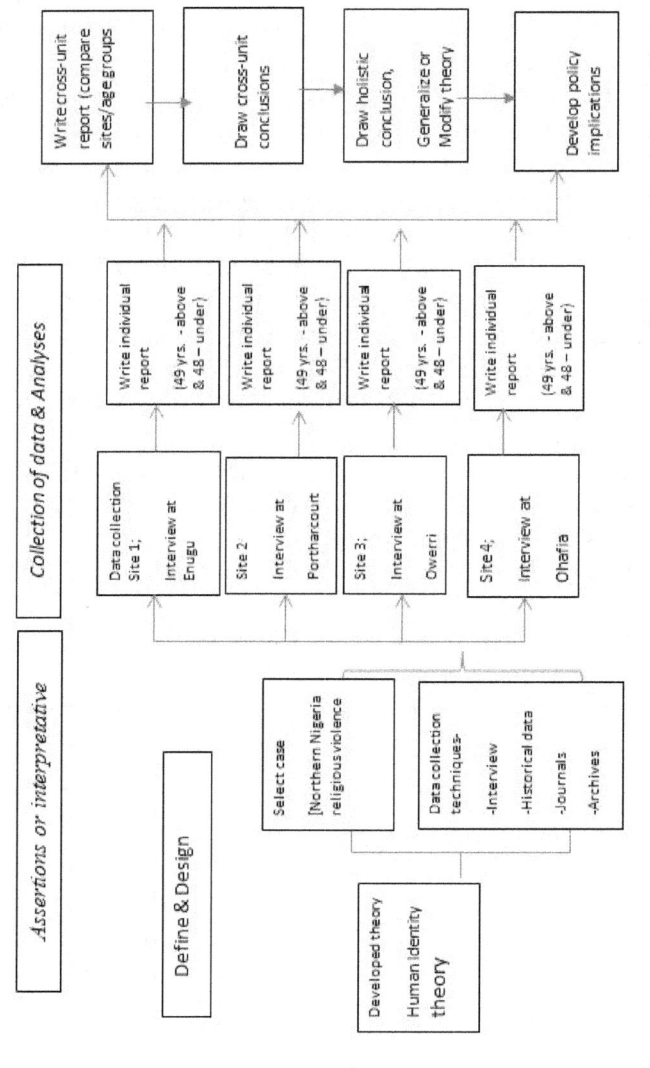

Figure 1. Flowchart of research process.

Validation Strategies

Validation in qualitative research "is an attempt to determine accuracy of the findings as described by the researcher and participants" (Creswell, 2007, p. 240). Validation questions whether the study can be replicated by another researcher based on data collection (Willis, 2007, p. 213). This study adopted Willis' methodological perspective for validation (Willis, 2007, p. 220). The research made use of different sources and theories to ensure corroboration of evidence.

Peer reviews from Nova Southeastern University, Florida, and external professionals helped to keep the researcher honest and ensured that all the right methods were used. Peer review which is a standard aspect of publication of scholarly journals by which suggestions and recommendations were made by scholars was attained (Willis, 2007, p. 221). Scholarly suggestions of the dissertation committee chair and two other members were obtained throughout the research process.

- I bracketed my biases from the onset of the study based on my past experiences (Willis, 2007, p. 221) with the Northern Nigeria violence that could impact the interpretation of the study.

- Data analyses, interpretation, and conclusions from this study were discussed with participants, especially leaders of the social groups as part of member checking to ensure accuracy and credibility of the account.

- External auditors were consulted to examine the findings, interpretations, and conclusions to ensure creditability and accuracy of the study.

The case study research validation that employs the use of primary source materials and one's knowledge to present understanding and descriptive writing of an event was done to create better understanding of the Northern Nigeria religious violence (Willis, 2007, p. 243). Other validation for scholarly research was attained through Creswell's (2007) standards of validation and evaluation of the research that questions:

  a)   Whether there is clear identification of the case under study

45

b)   If the case is used to understand the research issue, and have intrinsic merit

c)   Whether there is clear description of the case

d)   Are themes identified for the case

e)   Are assertions or generalizations made from the case analysis

f)   Is the researcher reflective or self-disclosing about the researcher's position in the study (Creswell, 2007, p. 219). (My bias and detailed experiences of research environment and study are disclosed in my role and background section.)

Role and Background of Researcher

I bracketed my bias from the onset of this study as a Nigerian from the Igbo Eastern Region that experienced most of the violence while living in different cities of Northern Nigeria (Creswell, 2007, p. 207). Although I attained my elementary and high school education within the Eastern region, I spent my holidays with my brothers who lived in Kano, Bauchi, and Jos. Each time school was on vacation I usually stayed with them so I could get my school fees to go back to school the next semester. After I completed my OND (Ordinary National Diploma), I also worked as a secretary in one of the major commercial banks. I had the opportunity of living in different cities of Northern Nigeria such as Bauchi, Jos, Kano, Minna, and finally Kontagora during these periods.

Within my twenty years of living in Northern Nigeria, I experienced waking up in the middle of most nights by the noise of my neighbors packing their luggage. When I inquired, one of them might be kind enough to whisper that they had information we (indigenous foreigners) might be attacked. Our place of escape was usually the military camps, government or public offices like the banks, and post offices were the violence was never extended. From the windows of these offices, we could see people walking down the streets with gallons of gasoline in their hands. Houses, stores, and churches were burned down as enchantments of Allah-akbar filled the air. People were slaughtered on the streets as they tried to run for

46

hiding. The commotion and attacks fade away at daylight or sometimes when the military intervenes and patrols the street or curfew is announced for restriction of movements at certain times of the night.

I am aware of my biases as a person from the Eastern region of Nigeria that witnessed several violent encounters in Northern Nigeria. I might be viewed as taking a particular side by readers, but I have written several papers on the negative influence of the colonial administration on Nigeria and benefits of multiculturalism in societies. For my undergraduate studies, my thesis was on "Multinational Corporations: Another Phase of Colonialism in Nigeria." I reenacted how most African countries including Nigeria received political independence from the colonial administration without economic independence. I researched on the activities of multinational oil corporations in Nigeria such as Shell, Elf, BP, and Agip. Their inability to help the country build and maintain working refineries so they would be able to process their oil products was stated as a control mechanism of the gas price and the economy. The corporations would rather enter into contract with the government to extract their oil, refine it, and sell it back to them with a sharing ratio of 60:40 without honorarium and development of their communities of operations.

As a doctoral student of conflict analysis and resolution, I have taken classes and acquired skills for analyzing conflicts from different perspectives. I have written papers on "Multicultural Awareness for Improved Relationship and Minimized Conflict," "Multiculturalism and Mediation," and a workplace training manual entitled "Diversity Awareness Training Program." I am aware of both sides and feel comfortable choosing this topic for my dissertation.

My concentration on Organizational and Schools Conflicts enabled me to dig into human and environmental factors contributing to the Northern Nigerian religious conflicts. During my classes in restorative justice we reviewed some of the strategies undertaken by most African countries such as South Africa as a result of colonial administration. The faith-mediation strategy by an Imam and a Pastor

47

in Kaduna came up in the case of Nigeria's religious violence. I listened to a video recording by the mediation practitioners about their efforts in using Mediation Practices to improve the Christian-Muslim relationships in the North. I listened to the struggles they were going through as conflicts continued to break out in the midst of the practices and other government strategies for restoring peace in Northern Nigeria. I recalled my childhood experiences and developed the passion to analyze the violence as ethnically related rather than religious for improved resolution strategies.

My passion as a student in different fields of study has been on the need for social justice and multiculturalism. I have come to believe over time that the things that unite us are more than the ones that divide us. The need for finding solutions to the causes of conflicts that relate to cultural differences is a goal in conflict resolution.

I am grateful to Nova Southeastern University and its lecturers for imparting this knowledge to me. I intend to utilize the skills acquired in conflict analysis and resolution to help organizations and societies improve their relationships, instill peace, and minimize conflicts. I am most grateful for the opportunity to analyze this inherent problem in my home country. Although I am not in any decision making position in Nigeria, I hope to use this opportunity to work with some faith-based organizations and social groups or present papers in different capacities to expand the consideration of this perspective for peacemaking in the state. By working with individuals, groups, organizations, and societies, I can help make the country more peaceful for our children.

Chapter 4

Data Presentation, Analysis & Interpretation

This chapter represents the data analysis of interviews, major federal government office cabinets and their officials, and military dispositions to determine the interconnectivity of struggle for power and resources that influence why the Igbo ethnic group suffers more in loss of life and property in major Northern Nigeria religious violence. Due to ongoing violence in most Northern Nigerian cities during data collection, the majority of the Igbo ethnic groups fled back to their Eastern region. Therefore, participants were selected and interviewed in four major cities within the Eastern region that includes Owerri (Imo State Capital), Enugu (Anambra State Capital), Portharcourt (Rivers State Capital), and Abia State rather than the proposed Northern cities. In-depth interviews were conducted with twenty-eight participants that lost family, friends, relatives, or properties in any of the violence while living in Northern Nigeria cities.

Participants were interviewed at their choice of location—mostly churches, business places, or homes. Their experiences covered numerous occurrences of violence in Northern Nigeria that includes the Sharia, Maitatsine, Beauty Pageant, Presidential elections, and other personal related attacks. All interviews were audio recorded without personal information or observation processes.

Demographics of Participants

A total of 28 interviews were conducted with Igbo ethnic groups that lived in major Northern parts of Nigeria. Participants' ages ranged from 24 to 70 years with four women and 24 men. Tables 1 and 2 represent the participants' respondents and economic background categorized by percentage distribution.

Table 1
Distribution of Participants

Age Group	Male	Female	Percentage
20-40	11	3	50
41-54	8	1	32.14
55 and above	5	0	17.86
Total	24	4	100

Source: Interview field 2014/2015.

Table 2
Economic Background

Profession	Number	Percentage
Students	1	3.571
Professionals/government workers	3	10.714
Religious Leaders	2	7.143
Traders	20	71.429
Others	2	7.143
Total	28	100

Source: Interview field 2014/2015.

Table 3

Summary of Participants' Loss and Answer to Why They Are Victims of the Northern Nigeria Violence

Participant S/N	Age	Sex	State of Origin	Loss suffered	Why they are victims	State/City of Residence
1	56	M	Enugu	Death of his wife and 3 kids (entire family)	Christian	Borno
2	56	M	Imo	Close friends/neighbors	Igbo	Nasarawa
3	56	M	Imo	Business, House & cars	Igbo	Nasarawa
4	47	F	Abia	House/2 cars	Igbo	Katsina
5	49	M	Abia	Friends and colleagues	Igbo/inequality	Kano
6	45	M	Abia	Home/properties burnt down	Igbo	Katsina
7	26	M	Abia	Friend	Wealthy Igbo/Christian	Kaduna
8	54	M	Imo	Gun shots to the face/properties	Igbo	Kaduna
9	70	M	Anambra	Friends, house, & properties	Igbo/cultural	Zamfara (Sokoto)
10	32	M	Imo	Friends, 2 stores, money & home	Christian	Plateau-Jos
11	24	M	Abia	Car & business	Igbo/Christian	Kaduna
12	46	M	Anambra	Brother, home, & business	Igbo/Christian	Kano
13	63	M	Imo	Properties & 38 years investments	Non-indigenous Christian	Yobe
14	31	F	Anambra	Business & properties	Igbo	Plateau-Jos
15	28	F	Imo	House, properties, & money	Igbo/Christians	Maduguri
16	29	M	Imo	Goods, shops, money, & home	Christians	Maduguri
17	26	M	Anambra	Brother, store, & properties	Wealthy Igbo men	Maduguri

18	42	M	Anambra	Brother & store	Christians	Kano
19	38	M	Imo	Friends, store, & home	Igbos	Kano
20	36	M	Imo	Brother, friends, neighbors, & business	Igbos	Kano
21	70	M	Abia	Church members	Igbos/political	Kaduna
22	36	M	Abia	Church members	Igbos/political	Jos
23	50	M	Imo	Bosom friend, 15 village members, water sachet industry, and car	Igbo	Adamawa
24	33	M	Imo	House, business, car, and bike (his entire livelihood)	Igbo	Adamawa
25	42	M	Imo	Friends, property, business, certificates, etc.	Igbo	Kano
26	30	F	Enugu	Home & business	Igbo	Kano
27	25	M	Imo	Brother, neighbors, & business	Wealthy Successful Igbo	Zaria
28	50	M	Imo	Family friend & business	Non-indigene, Political	Abuja

Source: Field Interview data.

Table 4
Data Unit Comparison of Violence Location

State	Number	Percentage
Kano	7	25
Plateau (Jos/Zaria/Kaduna/Nasarawa/Katsina)	12	42.857
Borno (Maidugiri/Yobe/Adamawa)	7	25
Others	2	7.143
Total	28	100

Source: Interview data 2014/2015.

Presentation of the Semi-Structured Interview

The interview presentation represented summarizes participants' answers to the question of why they think they were victims of Northern Nigeria violence and the loss they suffered (see appendix A). Participants' interview transcripts were summarized to capture their stories as they were victims of different violence experiences from 1960 to 2015.

Descriptive and In Vivo codes were applied to summaries, excerpts, and quotes that were directly taken from what the participants said (Saldaña, 2009). The choices for the codes' models are to help capture researcher's notes and participants' words to keep their stories close to original. Capitalized word(s) that describe participants' experiences and perceptions of the violence were placed on the right hand column with footnotes to explain the codes. Emerging patterns from codes were later merged to form research categories for further analysis.

Twenty-five percent of the participants interviewed indicated they lived in Kano at the time of violence. More than 42 percent lived in Plateau State that comprises Jos, Zaria, Kaduna, and Nasarawa. Nasarawa was carved out of Plateau State in 1996. More than 25 percent lived in the old Maiduguri State and Niger; Yobe was carved out of Borno State with Maidugiri as the state capital. All were in the Northeastern region. Only about seven percent indicated they experienced violence while living in other Northern states.

Kano, Kaduna, and Zaria created opportunities for major Igbo immigrants due to the construction of railway road lines in 1898 and 1912 that provided trading opportunities and better living conditions (ICG, 2010, p. 6). Although the cities are highly mixed ethnic populated areas, the groups have never been known to be integrated. Inter-ethnic violence between the Hausa-Muslims and Igbo-Christians like the 1953 protest rally that resulted to the killing of 200 Igbos continues to recur.

Appendix A: Participants Interview Summary

1. Participant one is a 56 year old man from Enugu in Anambra State that lived in the Bornu State of Northern Nigeria since 1973. [11]He had lost his entire family in one of the violence episodes: a wife, three children, home, and properties. [13]Two of his dead children had graduated from college while the last one was in high school. He began by narrating his experiences from the 1984 Maitaisine to 2001 Sharia in which he lost his friends and neighbors as well. [16]He started by stating he thinks the violence is religious-related since churches and not mosques were attacked and Christians and not Muslims were killed. He narrated the violence in which he lost his three children and wife in the 2002 violence. [11]He got emotional in the middle of his story and broke down for a while. [15]He later stated life has been unbearable for him since he lost all his properties. He is able to survive because of the help he is receiving from a church ministry in Portharcourt; he gets food and clothing from the pastor he calls daddy from time to time. [16]Although he suggested the violence is religious-related, when asked if there were other experiences he had before the violence to make him feel he	1LOSS 13 KILLINGS 16 ATTACKS IN CHURCHES 11 TRAUMA DUE TO LOSS 15 HARDSHIP DUE TO LOSS

was attacked because he is a Christian, he stated that during the violence [1]the alamagiris (beggars) always target Igbo people's properties like hotels, stores, and buildings and do not enter into properties owned by the Hausas. [12]

They went to Igbo stores; they broke them and stole their stuff. [1] Only Igbo hotels and houses were affected; they do not touch their own brothers or sisters.

I stopped the tape when his phone rang, and he needed to send the key to his extended family members to open the door. [9]He concluded by saying that he was continually called "cridi" (meaning people that do not know God) during Christmas festivals and on their way from church. To him, they were known as unbelievers and were attacked based on that assumption.

2. The second participant is 56 years old and lived in Adamawa state for over 25 years. [8]He experienced the Maitaisine violence in 1986 and stated they were slaughtering mostly the Igbos in Jamaitha (a city in Adamawa State). [20]He escaped into the bush with his family for three days. [13]However, his friends and neighbors were killed in the process. [11]He

12 BREAKING

1 JEALOUSY

9 NAME CALLINGS

8 COLONIAL SEGREGATION EFFECT

20 FLEE DUE TO FEAR OF EXTRADICTION

13 KILLINGS

19 ETHNIC

4 DISCRIMINATION

stated it was painful to see his friends die, but he was handicapped in helping them. To him he feels it is the job of the Nigerian federal government to bring a stop to the ordeal, and he was just grateful he did not die in the process. After the experience he decided to return to the East and has refused to go back to the North. [19]When asked why he thinks he is a victim of the violence, he stated it's because he is an Igbo man: [4]a non-indigene of the Hausa/Fulani in Northern Nigeria. When asked why he thought that was the reason behind the violence; he said he had no doubt because only Igbos were [10]targeted, and that the Yorubas or Hausas were not killed in the process. To him, sometimes other non-indigenes could become victims in the process, but the main focus is on Igbos; he said they enter the churches because they know Christians are dominated by the Igbos[19].	19 ETHNIC 20 FLEE FOR FEAR OF EXTRADICTION 21 HISTORICAL 11 LOSS/TRAUMA 15 HARDSHIP
3. The third participant is 56 years and worked as a civil servant in Mubi, Adamawa State for 32 years. He experienced lots of violence but narrated on the recent Boko Haram issue. He stated how he was coming back from his lecture job and noticed they were blocked in the middle of the road while driving home with his six-member family. [20]They abandoned their vehicles and ran into the bush to escape out of	19 ETHNIC

the state through the Cameroonian borders. [21] They camped in the city of Bermuda for days and were lucky to be helped by the Deeper Life Church vehicle that drove them to a place where they were able to get public transportation down to Eastern Nigeria. [11]He lost his two vehicles that were highjacked by the insurgents, his home, friends, and colleagues; he still feels traumatized whenever he hears sounds of gun shots or Christmas crackers. [15]He is yet to secure any job, and his kids have not been able to go back to school. He stated he lost properties for which he labored for more than 32 years and personal friends that were killed in the presence of their families. [19]He thinks he is a victim because he is of the Igbo decent, suggesting that the Igbos are generally targeted because they are hardworking and have incurred lots of properties in the North. [18]To him, the insurgents focus on churches because they know the majority of the Igbos are Christians. When asked if there were other experiences prior to the Boko Haram that made him feel he was targeted as an Igbo person, he said:

[19]We are victims because it is a religious issue, just because [19] ETHNIC we came from Igbo extraction. The stores of the Igbos were burnt down. We as Igbos are being targeted.

17 POLITICAL

19 ETHNIC

3 VIOLENCE-DOMINATION

1 JEALOUSY

4 DISCRIMINATION

3 VIOLENCE-DOMINATION

[1]Igbos are targeted because they are hardworking people.[1] JEALOUSY

[13] KILLINGS

[20] FLEE FOR FEAR OF EXTRADITION

He narrated the 2011 presidential riot in which Igbo people's stores and properties were destroyed after Goodluck Jonathan won the election. [8]To him, the Hausa Muslims are yet to accept the Igbos as full fledge Nigerians with the same rights as others since after the Biafran war.

[11] TRAUMA

[17]2011 when President Jonathan was declared winner, [21]They went out and burnt the stores, and beer parlors of the Igbos..... [3]It didn't go well with the Muslim leaders that minority won the election. [3]They wanted to hold down the presidency and since it is no longer in their hands, they generate Boko Haram to cause problems. [1]

[11] LOSS

When asked if he had other things to share in regards to the study, he suggested that the Igbos are not welcomed in the North because they are threats to the Northerners due to their hard work. [4]That they are virtually discriminated against in all sectors in the North including jobs and admission into schools and colleges. [3] To him a Northerner feels it is within their identity to rule the country, and losing the 2011 presidential election to a

[14] LOOTING

[11] LOSS

[16] ATTCKS IN CHURCHES

[1] JEALOUSY

Southerner brought about the Boko Haram violence.

4. The fourth participant is a 47 year old woman from Ohafia, Abia state that lived in Adamawa State for 23 years and lost all her properties in the violence. She began narrating the attacked that occurred in 2012 where Igbo people had gathered for a funeral ceremony of one of them that was killed in the city. [13]Suddenly there were gun shots in the bereaved man's house and about 12 other Igbo men were killed. [20]The crisis according to her prompted most Igbo people to flee the North and relocate to the East or send their immediate families home. The last one that caused her to leave the North was the 2013 Boko Haram in which she and her family spent days in the bush trying to escape out of the state. [11]She narrated how she had forgotten to take her son's insulin medication and nearly lost him because he was out of treatment for more than three days. She was able to get help at night in one of the cities and continued the journey with her weak son not knowing what will happen to him. She was grateful to get help in the Cameroons even though it was a different medication from the one the son had been on. [11]She lost their two vehicles and all the properties in their home.

10 TARGETING

5 ISLAMIC IDEOLOGY

4 DISCRIMINATION

1 JEALOUSY

5. The fifth participant is 49 years old from Abia and lived in Kano for 13 years when he was transferred to the region as a civil servant. He experienced the beauty pageant riot in 2000 that was later moved to London due to the crisis and a riot where Igbo properties were looted[14]. He lost his friends in both[11]. He feels the violence is more [1]due to envy of the Igbos because of some disparities between them Igbos and the indigenous Hausas, and Igbos properties are usually destroyed in the process. [16]He also felt it could be religious affiliated because of the riot that occurred during Reinhard Bonnke's visit to Nigeria and the Sharia crisis. [1]He, however, stated that no matter the reason for violence, the Igbos are always victims saying that [10]"each time the Northerners cough, the Igbos suffer." He also thinks it could be due to cultural differences and [1]inequality in wealth accumulation between the Igbos and Hausas. [5]According to him, he feels the Northerners do not want their people to be corrupted by the Christian religion or other ways of doing things like the pageant where people dress in their bikinis. He suggested that the inequality gap be breached to cut down on recurrence of the violence. [4]He thought he was a victim because of his dressing, language, and religion that is different from the Northerners.

5 ISLAMIC IDEOLOGY

6 ASSYMETRY

19 ETHNICITY

12 BREAKING/BURNING

7 ETHNICTY/RELIGION

17 POLITICAL

12 BREAKING/BURNING

15 HARDSHIP

I was a victim because of my mode of dressing and culture. [4]If I dress like them and speak like them, they will not know the difference.

[5] He thinks the Islamic religion that suggests followers that die during a Jihad war will inherit seven virgins in heaven ignites Muslims to violence. [1]He feels the Igbos are usually the object of attack because they are likened to the bourgeoisie of the place while majority of the Hausas are the peasants.

When they are begging we give them money...
[1]They believe all Igbo people are wealthy.
They believe the Igbos are far ahead in education so they say why don't we just stop it so we can all be at the same level.

The Hausas to him feel the Igbos exploit the wealth in their region to develop their own place. [1]They also feel the Igbos are more educated and they cannot catch up with them and think the best way of handling the difference is to destroy them. [11]Although he lost his friends and colleagues in the attack, he is grateful he was not killed in the violence. He advised the Nigerian government and Islamic religious leaders to eliminate the Alamagiris (beggars) and encourage more education in the North to bridge the inequality gap.

10 TARGETED

5 ISLAMIC IDEOLOGY

16 ATTACKS ON CHURCHES

10 TARGETED/TREATENED

[5]*Anybody reading the work should stop alamajiris, eliminate inequality, poverty, illiteracy. When they tell you to go and kill, you will not. [6]Education will bridge the gap between Rankadede (elites) and Alamagiris.*	20 FLEE FOR FEAR OF EXTRADITION
6. The next participant is a 45 year old man from Abia that lived in Funtua – Katsina State for about 18 years. He narrated his experiences of the introduction of Sharia law in the year 2000 and the pro-election crisis of 2011 when Goodluck Jonathan won the election. He stated that his home and many churches were burnt because they knew most Igbos are Christians.	16 ATTACKS ON CHURCHES
[19]*when it was announced that Jonathan won the election, [12]they took to the streets and burnt down all the churches [7]because they know most Igbo are Christians. All this while they have been ruling the country, there was nothing of that nature, but, [17]when they hear somebody from another part of the country won, they took to the streets[12]*	13 KILLINGS 20 FEAR OF EXTRADITION
He narrated how they surrounded his home with tires in the middle of the night and set it on fire. To him, it was by the grace of God that he broke down one of the walls at the back yard and escaped with his family. I had to re-record this experience as he began giving me	5 EXTERNAL/HISTORICAL

details after I had turned off the tape. [15]He stated he was angry because he became a refugee in his own country and is now living by the mercy of others because he exercised his voting rights. To him the Hausas have been ruling for a long period of time and the Igbos had no problem with that. [3]He wondered why it should be a problem because a Southerner won a Presidential election. He stated that the election was transparent as everyone lined up to vote. [4]He felt they noted who the Igbos voted for as they lined up at the polling booths. [10]They were marked as they jubilated when the result was announced. When asked why he thinks he is a victim of the violence he restated that it was because he is an Igbo indigene. [4]He stated that the introduction of the Sharia Law in a state with a mixed population was discriminatory since the Christians and the Muslims had nothing in common. He advised that the Igbos invest more within their states of origin to avoid more loss of their properties since the violence keeps recurring.

1 JEALOUSY

4 DISCRIMINAION

8 COLONIAL FAVORITISM EFFECT

7. The seventh participant is a 26 year old college student that witnessed his friend killed right before his presence. He was born in Zaria (Kaduna state) and had lived there with his parents all his years. He said he experienced several episodes of violence from

2000, 2006, and 2010. [5]He, however, lost his friend in the 2010 riot after the Muslim "Jumai" (Friday prayers). He felt his friend became a victim because he was dumb and refused to heed to his advice to turn back. [11]His friend was killed with the "langalanga", a curved kind of Machete for killing cows at the 2010 election riot when President Goodluck was declared the president of Nigeria. He escaped because he continually played dead and laid in the gutter each time he approached the rioters as he was running for his life. [16]Although he felt most of the crisis are religious related since they always attack churches, [10]he stated, however, that wealthy Igbo men are usually the target and they sometimes send them text messages or letters telling them to vacate their state or face being killed. [20]He stated his father and his friends got such messages and have since relocated back to the East.

8. The next participant is a 54 year old Igbo man that suffered gunshot wounds to his mouth during the Sharia violence in Kaduna. He moved between religious and political as the reasons behind the violence although he strongly stated it is religious related. He narrated a story on a riot that occurred during a Christian activity in which he was shot in the

| 4 DISCRIMINATION |
| 13 KILLINGS |
| 7 DISLIKE OF WESTERN VALUES |
| 10 TARGETING |

mouth. [16]The Muslims in Kaduna had taken to the streets prior to the riot chanting that Islam was the true religion. The next day the Christian Association of Nigeria (CAN) organized Christians to march through the streets of Kaduna stating their religion was a true one as well. [16]The Christians were, however, attacked by the Muslims, killing and burning most of them and their properties. [13]He was shot three times on the face, but the bullets all hit his mouth. He was scared to go to any of the hospitals within the city to extract the bullets. [20]Most Igbo people including himself decided to move back to Easterner Nigeria, and he has since not gone back. In his analysis of why he thinks he is a victim of the violence, [5]he suggested the attacks are instigated by foreigners from neighboring countries like Mali, Niger, Chad, etc., and not mostly by the Hausas in Northern Nigeria. [6]According to him, most of the government officials from the Northern Nigeria especially the military are not Nigerians. He suggested they migrated from those countries and have indigenized in Nigeria for a long period of time, and they are the ones instigating the crisis. [1]He also stated that an Igbo man naturally is hard working and likes to invest in properties while the Hausas are lazy and take life easy. To him, the Hausas are not happy that the Igbos come to their

16 ATTACK ON CHURCHES

5 ISLAMIC IDEOLOGY INFLUENCE

10 TARGETING

14 LOOTING

11 TRAUMA

20 FLEE DUE TO FEAR OF EXTRADITION

66

region and make lots of investment and because of that, they therefore do not want them in their region. [4]Continuous crisis in Kaduna, according to him, has prompted a division of State into Northern and Southern Kaduna in which the Muslims live in the North while the Christians dominate the South. According to him, the situation is synonymous to the overall Nigerian condition; the cost of living is cheaper within the Muslim region while it is expensive in the South. He also stated that he believes the violence is politically motivated; especially the Boko Haram issue and thinks the Igbo Chiefs and government officials are sleeping through the whole issue. [8]He stated that ignoring situations in which one of the states in the north, Sokoto State, had a vehicle plate sign with an inscription as "born to rule" signifies a strong message on the mind of the Northerners. According to him, people overlooked the situation for a long time until some people were able to connect it politically and the vehicle plate was put out of existence. However, many still use it. He thinks there should be no reason why a particular part of the society should feel it is their birth right to rule and others should not. He concluded that the country is divided into Muslims as the privileged and Christians/Igbos as the

5 ISLAMIC IDEOLOGY

15 HARDSHIP DUE TO LOSS

16 RELIGIOUS

12 BOMBING

19 ETHNIC

marginalized. [4]To him, the Muslims are free to say or do anything in the country and get away with it, but Christians and Igbos cannot.

4 DISCRIMINATION

9. The ninth participant is a seventy-year-old who lived in Zamfara state for 34 years. He experienced the Kaduna riot and the presidential riot of 2011 when Jonathan won the election. [20]During the violence he and his family ran to the army barracks and stayed for seven days based on the threat by the Hausas that they will destroy all Igbo people and their churches. [12]They burned a majority of the churches in the area warranting him to run for his life. [13]One of his friends was dragged out of his house and beheaded in front of his family. His other friend was able to escape by hiding in the ceiling of his house until the violence was over. [21]He thinks he is a victim of the violence because the Hausas always react against the Igbos in the North for virtually any global occurrence involving the Western and Muslim countries. [7]For example, he suggested there were riots in major Northern Nigerian cities during the USA Afghanistan and Iraq war and many Igbos were killed. [2]He stated that the Hausas do not want them in the North because they are not their brothers and do not do things the way they do. He concluded that the same behaviors are extended to Hausa-

11 TRAUMA

2 HATRED

9 NAME CALLING

13 KILLINGS

19 ETHNICITY

17 POLITICAL

3 VIOLENCE AS SCARE TACTICS

10 TARGETING

Christians with the exception of some Yorubas that are Muslims. When asked if other non-Igbos are affected during the violence, [10]he stated that although Igbo people and their properties are targeted, he is not sure how the violence impacts other non-Igbos personally. [16]However, when the churches are burnt down, it affects other non-Igbos as well. [5]He concluded by suggesting that the Islamic religion that promises members that they will be rewarded with seven virgins if they die in any jihad war highly influences the crisis. He pleaded for help to bring peace in the country in any possible way.

8 COLONIAL ETHNICIZATION

11 TRAUMA

10. Participant number ten is a 32 year old Igbo man from Mbaitoli in Imo State and lived in Jos, Plateau state for about 20 years. He experienced about three crises that included the 2001 market riot where he lost his business. He narrated how a cow was purposefully let loose in the market by the Fulanis to distract their attention. [10]To him, they thought it was a mad cow, and they all chased after it to stop it from damaging their properties. [14]It turned out, however, to be a set up as riots erupted from there and their goods were looted. [3]The most grievous to him was the January, 2010 Presidential riot in which he lost four of his friends and his two shops were

15 HARDSHIP

7 ASSYMETRY

3 DISCRIMINATION

burned down with about two million Naira worth of goods. [14]Another of his stores was looted with about 200,000 Naira cash taken away. He fought back to defend his goods, his family, and home from being destroyed, but he ended up losing them. [11]He said he did not want to recall the details of the violence because it is emotional for him. However, he stated that since he has been living in Northern part of Nigeria, he and his friends do not usually sleep at the same time. [20]They take turns staying up at night to watch out for break-out of any type of violence. [5]Chanting of "ila ila-ilala" usually fills the air before the attacks. [15]After losing his properties and business, he moved back to Eastern Nigeria where he got help from his church to restart his business. Although the business is small compared to what he had in the North, he is happy he can have peace and is no longer fearful for his life. [16]He concluded that the crises are religious related because he lost some of his friends that were Hausas too and blamed the political leaders for abusing the poor and not finding solution to the issue.

11. The next participant is a 24 year old that lived in Kaduna and Zaria state and experienced his church (CKC) being burnt down. [12]A bomb carrier exploded with the

19 ETHNICITY

2 HATRED

7 DISLIKE FOR
EDUCATION/WESTERN
VALUES

5 ISLAMIC IDEOLOGY
18 ETHNICITY

70

bomb beside his car causing him to lose it. [20]He made up his mind to leave the North and relocate back to the East when Igbo individuals that he knew were singled out and killed on daily basis. He became afraid and left, leaving his houses and other businesses. When asked why he thinks his friends were selected in the violence, [18]he stated that he was not sure why but they were, however, Igbos and Christians. When I probed on other common characteristics with his friends that were targeted, he stated they were [19]"people that were doing well in their businesses, mainly Igbos and Christians that are peaceful, have never in any way hurt anybody and usually mind their business." When it comes to the question of other behaviors he experienced before the violence, [4]he stated that the complaints or cases he had with Muslims were never processed in court and were usually ignored. [4]So personally he does not bother to follow up on anything or cases he has against Hausas/Muslims because it usually turns out to be a waste of time and he leaves it in God's care. [11]He concluded that he left his houses and properties because they were underpricing them when he tried selling them because they knew he would eventually abandon it. He is happy, however, that he can sleep without fear and does not mind his lost or abandoned

13 KILLLINGS

3 VIOLENCE AS SCARE TACTICS

4 DISCRIMINATION

2 HATRED

4 DISCRIMINATION

properties. He concluded by requesting that a solution be found to the problem in the North to allow everyone to live in peace.

1 JEALOUSY

12. The participant is 46 years old and lived in Kaduna, Kano, and other parts of Northern Nigeria. [2]According to him, the Hausa-Muslims hate Christians, and they are always referred to as [9]"infidels" meaning pagans who do not worship the true God. He narrated on the 2011 Presidential election crisis when Jonathan won the election. [13]However, the one that affected him was the Boko Haram issue in which his brother who worked at the bus station was killed in a bus stop bomb explosion. [19]The participant stated he strongly feels the violence is purely ethnic because a Hausa/Muslim man hates an Igbo man without any justification. [17]Towards the end he stated he also thinks the violence is politically related. [3]He thinks the political elites in the North are using the Alamagiris to influence violence, and non-indigenes/Christians are usually their targets[10]. He wondered why they complain about government inequality and end up attacking churches and non-indigenes' properties[3]. When asked why he thinks those are the reasons behind his experiences, he stated that he was always asked who his father is and whether where he lived was his place[8].

18 ETHNICITY

4 DISCRIMINATION

He finally relocated to avoid losing more of his family members.	1 JEALOUSY
13. Participant 13 is a 63-year-old man from Imo state who lived in Yobe State for 38 years and witnessed several violence episodes including Mataisine, Sharia, 2011 Presidential riot, and Boko Haram. The violence made him loose lives and properties. [16]To him, he thinks the violence is purely religious because they target only Christians and non-indigenes. [11]He stated how he has been stressed out by the crisis as they usually flee without knowing where they are going and what they might meet on their way. [8]However, they usually aim at getting to Plateau State where there are more Christians to determine if they need to get back to their location or proceed to the East. When asked how the violence has impacted him, his family, and friends, [15]he stated he left his properties and investments of 38 years to run for his life. [20]According to him, because he had been in the area for a long time and seemed to know the people behind the Boko Haram and the manner of Igbo people killed in the process, he felt he might be singled out.	18 ETHNICTY/RELIGION 1 JEALOUSY 19 ETHNICY 6 ASSYMETRY 19 ETHNIC 11 TRAUMA 3 VIOLENCE AS SCARE TACTICS
[7]*The head of Boko Haram is a degree holder but he does not want others to go to school. The equipment they use like telephone are*	20 FLEE FOR FEAR OF EXTRADITION

73

made by people that had education....[3]There are other things attached to it; the politicians are using them. Governor Ali Sherriff used them to win his election and even got elected the second term, that is why they gained ground...[19]	12 BREAKING/BOMBING
He stated that their targets are strangers and that he thinks the Igbos are victims due to their business success even though he began by stating the episodes of violence are purely religious. When asked why he said Igbo people and their properties are targets, he recounted how he eavesdropped on a discussion of a Northerner asking:	18 ETHNIC 2 HATRED 5 ISLAMIC IDEOLOGY
[2] *"why there were still Igbo people in the North when they were told they had been all killed during the Biafran War."*	
Other reasons why he thinks Igbos are targeted for the violence include cultural differences, influence of Western education, and Christianity. [7]According to him, a Hausa man does not want his culture corrupted by the Western ways of doing things. He suggested that could be the foundation behind the formation of Boko Haram explaining it to mean "Western education" is an "abomination."	3 VIOLENCE AS SCARE

74

[7]They said it is because of Western education their people have opened their eyes and are doing everything. They are however not saints, ehe, they do things in the hidden way; they drink but in the secret, they practice harlotry but in the secret. But Western education has made them to do things openly.

He thinks before the coming of Western education, the Northerners dressed in certain ways that will not expose their bodies and never allowed their women outside of the home. That to him explains the reason for their rioting at the world beauty pageant, and the kidnapping of the "Chibok" students in 2014 by the Boko Haram. [5]Other practices like drinking and prostitution are done in secret by the Northerners, however, [18]the Igbos drink in the open exposing their people to such practices that they despise. He also thought Boko Haram is politically instituted and feels they might have experienced conflicts with their leaders which resulted to their rampage killings. [13]To him the indiscriminate killings make it difficult to understand the aim of the violence. [3]However, he believes the northern political elites use the poor Hausas like the alamagiris, shoe shiners, money exchangers, etc., in perpetuating trouble for their selfish aims. [1]To him, they target successful strangers

TACTICS

10 TARGETING

16 RELIGIOUS

10 TARGETING

7 ASSYMETRY

3 VIOLENCE AS SCARE TACTIC

12 BOMBING

and burn their businesses. [3]He suggested the current Presidential candidate Muhammadu Buhari was behind the Boko Haram insurgents and intends to use them to help him win the upcoming elections in the North. According to him, he openly stated that he will make the office of President Goodluck Jonathan ungovernable if he won the 2011 election and it was written all over the local newspapers. He wonders why nobody did anything about it. [4]He concluded that there are lots of discriminatory practices on non-indigenes and Christians in attaining job or political positions in the North and the Igbos are always reminded of the Biafran War and how they were killed. When they protested against the use of identity cards in the state, some of them wrote in the paper saying:

[2]*"they should remember what happened in the North, that in the last one they killed Over 3 million Igbo people. [4]So they should decide whether they want the identity card or want that to happen again."*

Although he continually emphasized the violence is purely religious motivated, he kept moving between Christians and Igbos as victims. When asked to clarify his use of Christians or Igbos as targets of the violence,

10 TARGETING
11 TRAUMA
13 KILLINGS
13 KILLINGS
10 TARGETING
19 ETHNIC
11 TRUAMA
4 DISCRIMINATION
16 RELIGIOUS
9 NAME CALLING

[1]he explained that the Igbos are hardworking and their trading business takes them to different parts of the North. [3]The Northerners, on the other hand, mostly depend on government allocations and contracts and can hardly manage because they have numerous wives and children. According to him, the Northerners think the Igbo man exploits them through their business and they, therefore, are usually their object of targets in the violence. [7]He concluded, however, that there are different factors that could influence the violence including tribalism, religion, and politics. [8]To him, no matter the factor influencing it, the Igbo man, their families, and properties are always the targets for the violence. [4]He prayed for a solution to the crisis as it is a big problem, and he does not understand why the Hausas in the East are never disturbed while they keep disturbing others in the North. He concluded by suggesting a split of the nation to provide a solution to the problem if none can be found.

14. Participant 14 is a 31-year-old woman that was born in Zaria and had lived all her life there. She indicated experiencing lots of violence and recounted riots that occurred while she and her mother were pregnant simultaneously. [12]However, in 2012 a bomb

10 TARGETING/ TREATENING

18 ETHNIC/POLITICAL

2 HATRED

3 VIOLENCE/DOMINANCE

13 KILLINGS

14 LOOTHING

12 BREAKING/BURNING

18 COLONIAL SEGREGATION

10 TARGETED

18 ETHNICTY/RELIGION

blast occurred in their church while she was still getting ready at home. She was happy she escaped it, and therefore decided to relocate to the East thereafter and is not sure if she will be going back to the North in the near future. She indicated she suffered loss of her properties and businesses that has made life financially difficult for her and her family. When asked why she thinks she is a victim of the violence, [1]she unequivocally stated that each time there is misunderstanding between other races or any form of violence in Northern Nigeria, the Igbos are usually attacked[18]. According to her, a Northerner thinks the Igbos came to the North to enrich themselves and therefore do not want them there.

[1]In the Northern area, anytime there is fight, even if it is between Yoruba and Hausa, they attack the Igbos because they think they have come to take their money and enrich themselves.

I had to stop the tape in the process of the interview to allow her attend to her customers as the interview was held at her shop (place of business). On the question of why she thinks she is a victim of the violence, she stated it is because of her ethnicity as an Igbo person[19]. She narrated an incidence in which her sister

8 COLONIAL

18 ETHNICTY/RELIGION

19 ETHNICITY

18 ETHNICY/RELIGION

78

was attacked in her school because she is so smart and usually answers most questions in class[6]. She also stated that they only burn the churches and shops owned or attended by the Igbos. [19]According to her, those of the Yorubas and other ethnic groups are never affected and that made her to strongly believe that the Igbos are the main target of the violence. She prayed for solution to the violence.

13 KILLINGS

8 COLONIAL SEGREGATION EFFFECT

15. The next participant was a 28-year-old pregnant woman from Anambra State. [11]She was highly emotional in recounting her ordeal in the violence that I pleaded with her to allow me stop the interview, but she insisted on continuing. [3]She narrated her experience in the 2009 violence that occurred in the market in which she ran to the barracks while three months pregnant. [20]They stayed in the barracks for over seven days at the mercy of the soldiers and Reverend Fathers without food or clothing.

[12]She also talked about the ongoing Boko Haram bomb explosions that occurred on her way from the hospital while pregnant. She and her family finally fled to the East abandoning their properties and businesses in the North. She could not say for sure why she thinks she is a victim of the violence but suggests it could be due to her religious affiliation as a

10 TARGETED

7 DISLIKE FOR EDUCATION/WESTERN VALUES

Christian. When asked the characteristics of those she witnessed killed or who lost their properties, [18]she indicated they were mostly Igbos as well as some Hausas that are Christians. [2]She thinks Hausa-Christians are targeted as well because of their association with the Igbos.

11 LOSS

On the question of other experiences she had gone through before the violence, [5]she indicated that Hausa alamagiris and shoe shiners on the street are generally unfriendly and violent to non-indigenes. [10]She stated that living in the area as a woman is very risky as they are continually raped and threatened to be killed. [4]Complaining or fighting back could start violence. [19]She concluded by stating that the Igbos are the major targets; however, the Christian-Hausas could be affected because they are seen as associating themselves with the Igbos. [11]Since she was highly emotional in recounting the experiences and was pregnant with another child, I had to skip some of the questions to cut the interview short.

10
TARGETING/TREATENING

19 ETHNIC

3 VIOLENCE AS SCARE
TACTICS

4 DISCRIMINATION

8 COLONIAL/PRE-
BIAFRAN

16. Participant 16 is a 29-year-old boy from Imo State and was born in Zaria and had lived there all his life. He narrated his experience of the 2011 Presidential riots. [3]He stated the Northerners indicated that a Christian will not

rule them. [12]They therefore took to the streets burning houses, shops, and other business places. [10]Later came the Boko Haram bomb blast at the "Sabon Gari" (non-indigenous quarters) where he lived. [11]He lost his goods, shops, finances, and home and decided to flee back to the East to start life afresh. [16]To him, he thinks the violence is religiously associated because he was always pressured to become a Muslim at his store located close to the Emir's palace. [3]When asked why he thinks that is the reason for the violence, he recounted listening to the Northerners saying that Nigeria cannot be ruled by Christians and that only Muslims are destined to rule the country. [10]He stated how the perpetuators of the violence were going from store to store to shoot people. [7]According to him, they concentrated their actions in schools and Christian gatherings, and therefore, lots of students and Christians lost their lives in the process. When asked why he thinks they chose those places, [3]he stated he overheard the Muslims saying they will continue to ferment trouble as long as the current president Jonathan Goodluck continues to be in power because the Muslims are born to rule while the Christians are meant to do business.

10 TARGETING

5 ISLAMIC IDEOLOGY

19 ETHNIC

15 HARDSHIP

16 RELIGIOUS

3 VIOLENCE/DOMINATION

17. The next participant is from Anambra State, is 26 years old, and lived at Maduguri since 2007. He experienced the Boko Haram violence that has been recurring since 2009. [12]For four days from Monday to Thursday, bomb explosions continued to occur in his area, and he witnessed some occur right in his presence at the custom area where lived[10]. He was also highly emotional in recounting the stories and did not want to relive the experience[11]. He stated he could not collect the money from the supplies he made and lost his brother who was shot at his store while his uncle quickly disposed of his building properties to flee back to the East. He stated he was not sure why he is a victim of the violence. [13]In asking him to describe the people that were mainly affected by the violence, he stated they were successful Igbo businessmen. [13]He gave example of his father's friend that his two sons who were killed because he refused to show up from his hiding place when the Boko Harams came to his house. [10]They demanded that he come out or risk his sons being killed; when he hesitated, his two sons were killed. He finally concluded that all the victims he witnessed were all Igbos[19].

6 EXTERNAL INFLUENCE

6 EXTERNAL INFLUENCE

10 TARGETED

6 EXTERNAL INFLUENCE

12 BOMBING

18. The next participant is a 42-year-old man from Anambra State that lived in Kano State for almost 22 years. He stated experiencing a series of violence episodes in the North including the ongoing Boko Haram and decided to flee to help save his family[20]. He however lost a relative in a church bomb blast who later died while receiving treatment in the hospital[11]. He wondered if Nigeria is really one due to the treatment they receive as non-indigenes there[4]. He lost his properties and money[11]. He tried selling his property and nobody would buy them. [16]He believes the violence are religious related and thinks the Muslims in the North do not want to associate with Christians whether from the Igbo or anywhere. [9]They are called unbelievers, and they intend to turn the country into a Muslim country. [10]He stated that he continually received threats that non-Muslims should leave the area or they will be killed. [18]In answering the question of why he thinks those are the reasons behind the violence, he stated that during elections, those that vote for Christians are usually eliminated (killed). He suggested that Christians or Muslims that support Christians are always targeted in the violence. [2]Muslims only become victims if they try to support or help the Christians.

2 HATRED

19 ETHNIC

18 ETHNIC/REGLIGION

1 JEALOUSY

2 HATRED

5 ISLAMIC IDEOLOGY

16 RELIGIOUS

13 KILLING

10 TARGETING

10 TARGETING

[3]They say Christians are ruling and anything about Christian they don't like it.... See in 2011 election, the man got a lot of votes from the North, and they said it is not supposed to be so. [13]So they said if you vote for a Christian they will eliminate you, so I just wonder how this election will be there...	19 ETHNIC 2 HATRED
[14]According to him, shops belonging to Christians irrespective of whether they are from the North or East are targeted. He stated that the government and the press are not giving a true picture of the killings and what is going on in the North. He asked that a proper representation be made so the world can know what is going on.	19 ETHNICITY 10 LOSS 20 FLEE DUE TO FEAR OF EXTRADITION
19. Participant 19 is 38-years-old from Imo State, and lived in Kano State for more than six years. He experienced the recent Boko Haram violence within the Sabon-Gari quarters where he lived[10]. He lost his friend who was a bus worker at a bomb blast[11].	12 BOMBING 10 TARGETED 15 HARDSHIP
[12]I just heard a sound "boom!" three times... [18]They said Boko Haram have entered Sabon-Gari and bombed the place[10].	
	2 HATRED

He also recalled a church bomb explosion that killed another of his friends with many lives and cars destroyed.

[18]Their mission is to catch the souls of our Christian brothers; mainly Igbos… It usually happens where we Christians are gathered, Igbos are gathered …[8]It happens in our environment – Sabon-Gari, not theirs.

[20]He fled back to the East leaving his properties and businesses behind. He stated that starting life over has put him and his family in financial hardship. [18]He thinks Christians, mainly Igbos, are usually targeted because the insurgents focus on Igbo group gatherings. When asked why he thinks those were the reasons behind the violence, he suggested that the Hausas and Muslims do not show any sympathy when the violence occurs and they usually laugh at them when they happen. When asked to clarify between Christians and Igbos and if Hausa Christians with stores in his neighborhood are also targeted, he stated that when he says Christians he means Igbos because [19]the violence only occurs within Igbo residences and places of businesses. He pleaded for the world to know what is going on and for a solution to be found for the violence.

19 ETHNIC

18 ETHNIC/RELIGION

1 JEALOUSY

10 THREATENED/TARGETED

11 TRAUMA

2 HATRED

10 TARGETED

20 FLEE FOR FEAR OF EXTRADITION

12 BOMBING

20. The next participant happens to be the cousin to the former and is 36 years old and lived in Kano since 1997 but relocated back to the East in 2014. [18]He stated the violence he experienced in Kano were all targeted towards eliminating the Igbos from the Northern part of Nigeria although he started by suggesting Christians were the targets. [16]In recounting his experience he said they were attacked while at the church but luckily he had left earlier that day to attend to some personal business. [3]He referred to the Boko Haram violence as terrorist and politically related. According to him, he made the statement because he does not know why the Nigerian military that has helped other African countries in their wars are unable to handle the Boko Haram issue.

[3]The Nigerian military that I know used to go to ECOMOC and Sierra Leon to help them fight and win their battle, but this common Boko Haram they cannot handle it because it has entered politics.

[13]He suggested the Boko Haram insurgents started by killing Nigerian military officials and later to churches and now individuals. [8]He stated that the Muslims in his area usually say that the Christians and Muslims should not be mixed together and should be separated. When

13 KILLINGS	
7 DISLIKE FOR WESTERN VALUES	
17 POLITICAL	
3 VIOLENCE/DOMINATION	
1 JEALOUSY	
15 HARDSHIP	
3 VIOLENCE/DOMINATION	

asked of personal experiences he had heard prior to the riots that made him conclude that he is a target because of his religion, [4]he stated that the Igbos are usually treated as outcasts and the Northerners are looking for ways to make them go back to the East. To him, he cannot find words to describe the ill treatments and discriminations against the Igbos in the North and suggested for a split of the country as a solution. When asked to clarify why he is actually a victim of the violence in the North, [2]he stated the Hausas are always looking for an excuse to hurt the Igbos even when a conflict is externally related like the Afghanistan issue. [10]The Igbos to him are usually the target because 90 percent of the indigenous are foreigners in the North. [7]They and the Igbos are viewed as supporting Western and Christian values which the Northerners detest. He was very grateful for the opportunity to tell his story and pleaded for a solution to the violence as it makes the country unsafe.

21/22. These participants were two Igbo pastors with a mega church in different cities of the north. [11]They lost members of their church that they refer to as their sons and daughters. I decided to combine their analysis because they refused to be audio recorded stating their voices can easily be identified.

The first turned 70 years on the day of interview (January 1, 2015) and the other is 36 years old. [10]They both stated having been shortlisted for elimination because their ministry offers assistance to the families of the victims of the violence. [19]The 36-year- old pastor suggested different violence is formulated for the purposes of eliminating Igbos from the North and preventing them from assuming federal leadership positions. [3]He questioned why the majority of the violence occurs mostly in APC (All Progressive political Party) affiliated Northern states. [3]He stated the Igbos are killed in those states to stop and scare them away in order to stop them from voting for their political candidates and winning elections in those states. [4]The 70-year-old pastor concluded that it is difficult for an Igbo person to hold any political appointment without having him surrounded by Hausas or Yoruba ethnic candidates. [8]Both believe the same discriminatory actions that led to the Biafran War have continued to linger on and that the Igbos do not have equal rights like other ethnic groups and are yet to be accepted as Nigerians.

23. The next participant is a 50-year-old man from Imo state who lived in Mubi, Adamawa state for about 30 years. He experienced the

Mataisine, 1993 Abiola Presidential riot, and 1989 riot. [10]The riot claimed about 10 Igbo people in a funeral function. In all the violence, he stated Igbos lost lives and properties. [5]According to him, the Sharia crisis did not affect them much in Mubi because their Emir did not support it. [6]He questioned why his state needs to be Islamized and suggested that the foreigners from Chad, Niger, etc., who are pushing it should first establish it in their countries. He narrated on how people were targeted individually and killed in the ongoing Boko Haram violence. [19]To him he thinks the Igbos are the targets for the Boko Haram. However, he thinks somewhere along the line they experienced conflicts within themselves and some of their members decided to withdraw from the membership which resulted in the killing of other Muslims. [15]He stated life has been very difficult for him and his family financially because he lost all his properties and sachet water producing business and has not been able to recover. [15]He has been unable to put his kids back to school because he could not afford their school fees. [16]When asked why he thinks he is a victim of the violence, he stated because he is not a Muslim. [3]He stated his neighbor told him that the only solution to the violence is to ask the present President Jonathan to step down from office—[3]that only the Muslims can be presidents in Nigeria and others can assume other positions. [17]He thinks all violence in the North is directed towards frustrating Igbo people and their efforts towards ascending to the Presidential office in the country. [18]He suggests the reason why churches are targeted is because they know the majority of the Igbos are Christians. According to him, there have never been any bomb explosions in any Mushilashi (Islamic evening gatherings). [6]He concluded by stating that his Northern Muslim friends are generally nice and thinks they are influenced by outside immigrants from neighboring countries like Chad, Niger, Mali, Sudan, etc.[6]

24. I walked into this participant while he was undergoing a welcoming ceremony to the market from his store neighbors. He presented soft drinks (soda) and cabin biscuits (cookies) to them. They prayed for business success and good health for the new member after which they shared the drinks and ate the cookies. He stated he had lived in Adamawa State for over 15 years and is 33 years old from Imo State. [11]He lost his house, business, cars, and bicycles. His business was mostly affected by the current Boko Haram violence. [10]He narrated how young girls were raped, while elderly women and young men were

slaughtered with machetes before their families. [6]He stated that usually they hold markets on Tuesdays and Thursdays at Yobe border (the capital of Adamawa state) in which neighboring countries like Chad, Niger Republic, and others come to buy and sale. [12]On that particular day, bombs suddenly began to explode and people were killed in great numbers including Nigerian military men. When asked the description of people that were mostly killed, he stated they were mostly family men known to him. Some of them were taken away for several days and later returned. On the question of why he thinks he is a victim of the violence he states:

[2]*I don't know if it is a kind of hatred for Igbos, any kind of thing that happens, they put it on the Igbos[19]. They put bombs in churches because Igbos are there[18]. I don't know why they have this hatred.*

[1]He suggested Igbo people developed the region and have a lot of properties in the North, and he thinks there is some form of hatred from the Muslim-Hausas towards the Igbos who are mostly Christians[2]. When asked if there are other experiences he had from his Muslim neighbors before the violence, he suggested a Hausa Muslim is generally

friendly but can turn against them during violence.

These Muslims they are very friendly but they can attack you anytime. [5]They listen to their friends, neighbors and religion ...

25. The participant is 42 years old from Imo state and lived 27 years in Kano. [16]He experienced lots of violence including that of 1991 when Reinhard Bonnke visited Kano, and the 1994 riot. [13]Violence erupted because an Igbo man was beheaded for allegedly cleaning his bottom with a Koran leaf after using the toilet. [10]He stated the allegation was leveled on the Igbo person without stating any witnesses or given the opportunity to face trial. [4]The case was still in court when some Hausas publicly beheaded the man causing the Igbos to go to the streets to demonstrate against the treatment. [3]He also experienced numerous Presidential riots including 1999 when Abiola from the South won the election and Jonathan's 2010 election. [10]He stated his home and all apartments surrounding the area were demolished during the Jonathan crisis, and he decided to run back home. He has been in the East for a month. [1]He stated he was highly successful in his business at Northern Nigeria and feels sad recalling the stories surrounding

his down-fall. [19]According to him, he is a target because he is an Igbo man. [2]He stated the treatment has been in existence since the times of his father, and he too has experienced it. [19]According to him, it is not a secret that the Igbos are targeted—"it is glaringly clear." [10]He lost his friends, house, property, business, certificates, etc., and had to start from nothing. [20]He concluded that living in the North is a fearful and restless life and that a majority of the Igbos are asking their families living in the North to come back to avoid losing them.

26. The next participant is a 30-year-old woman from Enugu State that lived in Kano for seven years. [12]She mostly experienced the Boko Haram violence and lost her closest friend in a bus stop bomb blast earlier in the year. [10]The bombing continued around her business and residential area. She lost all her investments and belongings. [15]She says she is financially handicapped and can hardly make ends meet with her family. [2]She believes the Hausa Muslim hate the Igbos and all events are meant towards destroying them and in the event others become victims. When asked why she thinks she is targeted, she stated she is not sure, stating she usually lives amicably with her neighbors. [10]She wonders why violence usually occurs in the area:

[2]I don't know, is it a kind of hatred for Igbos? [19] Any kind of thing that happens, they put it on the Igbos. [18]They put bomb in the church because the Igbos are there. [2]I don't know why they have this hated.

She hopes peace will return to the area one day so she can relocate back as the cost of living is low and makes it easier for her to take care of her family.

27. The participant is a 25-year-old man that was living with his brother in Zaria and witnessed bombings at an Igbo wedding ceremony and his church. [1]He stated wealthy Igbo people that are successful in their businesses are the targets. [10]They always receive threatening letters, and they end up being killed either at their business places or at home. [11]He narrated how he lost all his Igbo neighbors and his brother that attended the wedding ceremony. [11]He was very nervous talking about his experiences and got the questions mixed up. On the question of why he thinks he is a victim he stated:

[2]So this people - the problem is that they hate Igbos and they Plan to destroy them, unfortunately other people are affected. [10]The day they thought the Igbo people are going

back they threw bomb at the park and many
people were affected.

However, he stated he was happy to be back to the East alive[20]. To him he thinks it is all in God's plan so they can invest and do business in their area.

28. This last participant is a 50-year-old man and is from Imo State. He lived in Niger State (Abuja) and narrated his experiences of much violence. [12]A church bombing claimed the life of his friend and his entire family in a church gathering. [13]The wife of his friend was spared because she did not go to church that day. Other violence narrated was related to the recent Boko Haram issue. [7]He explained Boko Haram to be a group protesting against Western influence in northern Nigeria and sees the Igbo man as a representative of those characteristics. [5]Boko as he explained means "Western" and Haram is "sacrilege" (abomination). [7]He cited how his Muslim-Hausa neighbor was warned that his brother should never dress in shorts in the compound or he will make his life unbearable. [17]He also suggests the violence is politically related. [3]He explained the violence is aimed towards hindering the Igbos from ascending to the Presidential positions in Nigeria.

[3]You know they have been governing for many, many years ...Jonathan won an election against a northerner – Buhari. They believe the election ought to be won by their brother. They feel they have taken the leadership out of their hands and they want it back by all means.

[1]He lamented on how wealthy he was with chains of businesses and investments in the North. [15]According to him, he can hardly make up to a dollar equivalent a day to take care of his family. [3]According to him, the purpose of Boko Haram is to make the country ungovernable because a Southerner (Jonathan) won the election. [3]He suggested the past Nigerian President Muhammad Buhari and current Presidential candidate made a statement publicly that he will make Nigeria ungovernable for President Jonathan and wonders why he has not been questioned. He is, however, optimistic that a solution will be found to the situation one day so the country can be at peace again.

Code, Categories, and Themes

Emerging patterns based on participants' perception on why Igbo people are victims of the violence include:

1.	Jealousy for Igbos' success in business/investments in the North based on targets of wealthy Igbo businessmen for violence and threats.

2.	Hatred based on the past Biafran War interpreted from participants' suggestions that the Hausa-Fulanis wondered why there were still many Igbos in existence when they thought they were all killed during the war.

3.	Northern elites' use of violence as scare tactics for winning elections in 12 Northern states for continuous domination of federal power.

4.	Discrimination in access to jobs, justice, and education to frustrate and stop Igbos' progress.

5.	Influence of Islamic ideology that promises members that die for the cause of Jihad war to inherit seven virgins in heaven.

6.	External influence from neighboring/historical countries of Chad, Mali, Sudan, etc., for a possible Islamization of the country based on participants' suggestions that the violence is externally influenced.

7.	Hausa-Islamic dislike for education and Western values represented in Igbos.

8.	Colonial segregation of foreign indigenous immigrants in Sabon-Gari quarters that formed areas of concentration for violence during from pre-Biafran conflicts.

9.	Name calling like cridi, capri, infidel, etc., to humiliate and frustrate the Igbos.

10.	Targeting and threatening of wealthy Igbo men by sending them text messages and notes to leave the North or be killed.

11.	Trauma associated with loss of loved ones and properties.

12.	Breaking of stores, as well as burning and bombing of churches and homes during violence.

13.	Killings of Igbos in great numbers during violence.

14.	Looting of shops and properties during violence.

15. Hardship associated with loss of properties, business, and relocation.
16. Violence assumed to be religious because of attacks in churches.
17. Violence assumed as political due to occurrences during Presidential elections and Southern candidates win.
18. Ethnicity and religion simultaneously used as reason for violence.
19. Ethnicity stated as reason for violence following participants' suggestion that the Igbos are targeted.
20. Flee to the military barracks or back to the East region due to fear of extradition based on pre-Biafran experience.

Categories and themes emerging based on the interview analogical analysis include:
1. Colonial Effect and Hatred from the past
- Pre/Post Biafran War age analysis
2. Interrelationship of Religion, Ethnicity, and Political Violence
- Psychological effects
3. Violence as Northern Tactics for Dominance of Federal Power
- Federal Government Cabinets' analysis in regions/religious groups
- Domination of Federal Power/Military; a Northern birth-right
4. Fight for National Cake; Federal Corruption/Misappropriation of Public Fund.

Colonial Effect/Hatred from the Past

A pre- and post-Biafran War age table was created to seek similarities in participants' views born before and after the Biafran War. Theoretical review suggests pre-war violence was based on Northern long resentment of Igbos' success in commerce and education (Mudimbe, 2013, p. 674). During the 1967 Hausa-Northern retaliation coup preceding the Biafran War, Igbos were sought in their homes and places and businesses and killed in great numbers. Sabon-Gari residence (foreign indigenous quarters) created by the European government became concentrated areas of attack (ICG, 2010, p. 5). The massive killings of Igbos described by Chinua Achebe as genocide intended to wipe the Igbos from the geographical map of Nigeria caused them to flee back to their region to regroup for the war. Table 5 indicates participants' perception of the reasons why they think they are victims of the violence in the North.

Table 5

Pre/Post Biafran War Age Analysis on Why They are Victims

Pre-Biafran War Age Group (before 1967)			Post-Biafran War Age group (after 1967)		
Partic-ipant S/N	Age	Why they think they are victims	Partic-ipant S/N	Age	Why they think they are victims
1	56	Religion	4	47	Ethnic
2	56	Ethnic	7	26	Ethnic/Religious
3	56	Ethnic	10	32	Religious
5	47	Ethnic	11	24	Ethnic/Religious
6	49	Ethnic	12	46	Ethnic/Religious
8	54	Ethnic	14	31	Ethnic
9	70	Ethnic/Religion	15	28	Ethnic/Religious
13	63	Ethnic/Religion	16	29	Religious
21	70	Ethnic/Political	17	26	Ethnic
23	50	Ethnic	18	42	Religious
28	50	Ethnic/Political	19	38	Ethnic
			20	36	Ethnic
			22	36	Ethnic/Political
			24	33	Ethnic
			25	42	Ethnic
			26	30	Ethnic
			27	25	Ethnic

Source: Interview data 2014/2015.

Based on the interview analysis above, six out of 11 of the participants born before the war think the violence is ethnically related while four think it is a combination of race and religion. Nine out of 17 participants born after the Biafran War think they are victims of the violence because of their race, and five said it is a combination of race, religion, or politics. Only three participants (one from pre-war and two from post-war age) think it is purely based on religion. Overall 89 percent of the participants think the violence has some ethnicity relativity.

Those that suggested the violence was both ethnic and political based their assumption on the 1999 and 2011 Presidential riots in which violence occurred because Southerners won the election. The current Boko Haram uprising was also assumed to be politically related and aimed towards frustrating and hindering the re-election of President Goodluck Jonathan. Participants 8, 13, 20, and 28 explained the intention of Boko Haram is to eliminate the Igbos who they see as a representative of Western culture due to their dressing, education, and religion as Christians. A majority stated that irrespective of the reason for violence in the North, Igbos are targeted. Participant 13 stated his neighbor wondered why the Igbos were still visible in the North when he had the impression they had been totally eliminated during the Biafran War. Their explanations seemed to align with Chinua Achebe's perception that the Biafran War was a genocide that was intended towards wiping the Igbos from the face from the earth.

Inter-relativity of Ethnicity, Religion, and Political Violence

Religion and ethnicity were interchangeably used by participants in their explanations of reasons for violence. Although some began by stating the violence episodes were religiously related, somewhere along the line they indicated they were victims because they were from the Igbo ethnic group, Christians, or non-indigenes of the Hausa-Fulani's decent living in Northern Nigeria. Religion and culture in Nigeria, like most African countries, are interrelated (Avruch, 1998). It becomes difficult to separate cultural norms and values from religious laws in Muslim-dominated countries such as Northern Nigeria. This practice may, however, differ according to countries due to their historical backgrounds and experiences. However, the three major regions in Nigeria are dominated by a particular religion.

The Christianity and Islam are the two major religions practiced in Nigeria. About 95% of the Northern Hausas practice Islamic religion while 5% are Christians (Pew Research Center, 2011). Ninety-eight percent of the Igbo dominated Eastern regions are Christians with about 2% practicing traditional or other religion; the Yorubas and others in the Southwest are made of about 55% Muslims and 35% Christians (Pew Research Center, 2011).

The same encyclopedia notes that Nigeria is the largest Muslim population in sub-Saharan Africa (Pew Research Center, 2011). Since religion and culture are interwoven, it becomes difficult to separate these ethnic groups from their religion of practice as it forms a major part of the people's identity. This could explain why religion and ethnicity were used in the descriptions of the regions; Hausa-Muslims or Igbo-Christians were continually used. Participants also used religion and ethnicity inter-changeably as the reasons why they were victims of the violence.

Stein (2011) believes religious differences can lead to conflict due to the central role it plays in constituting individual and group identity (p. 8). Religion similar to other components of ethnicity shapes people's belief and behavior. The importance individuals or society attach to their religion and how they think relationship with God should be is assumed to contribute to the role religion plays in conflicts.

Religion is a crucial component of cultural heritage and groups tend to place more importance on religion than their backgrounds or origins (Stepaniants, n.d.). Stepaniants suggests the "interconnections between sharing the same religious belief and ethnicity or nation in Islam is not dimensional" (p. 1). A state in Islam is regarded as a religious community and common religious belief establishes common ties more than tribal kingship. Based on Prophet Muhammad's experiences and Koran teachings, solidarity for people is established based on belief in Allah.

The community of the Prophet Muhammad's followers created in Medina Hijira (622) included both muhajirun and ansar. The muhajiruns were the Meccans who made the journey with Prophet Muhammad and were therefore accepted as inhabitants of Medina that accepted the authority of Muhammad, the umma were regarded as part of the community... tribal kinship was established based on common religious beliefs. (Stepaniants, n.d., p. 1)

Again, solidarity or loyalty towards Islamic ideology was also established in the Arabic history where they were asked to follow Allah and that those that followed asabiyya were not part of the community (Stepaniants, n.d., p. 1). In the interviews, respondents continually stated how they were referred to as infidels or 'cridis' by their Muslim-Hausa Northern neighbors when they are coming back from church. Participant 15, a 28-year-old woman, narrated how they are disrespected, assaulted, and raped openly by the almagiris if they walked the streets without covering their bodies like the Muslims. Respondents such as participants 5, 9, 11, and 13 suggest violence was instigated based on Islamic teachings that suggest followers will be rewarded with seven virgins in heaven if they die in a Jihad war. Participant 10 strongly maintained he was a victim because of his religion and because his Christian Hausa friends were also victims but could not recall if they were also attacked at home or at their respective business places. He said he drew his conclusions because his friends were also affected when the churches were burnt.

The Bangura (1994) states ethnicity can constitute a problem where "a state is the medium for modernization and such a nation is not what the various ethnic groups would have wished" (p. 9). The European government operated different offices and policies in Nigeria even after the amalgamation of North and South. The literature review indicated violence began to break as far back as in 1957 in protest over the amalgamation of the North and South. Crisis also broke out amongst the Northern ruling Sokoto Qadiriyya and Tijaniyya brotherhood over the Westernization of the caliphate by some of their political leaders. Participants 4 and 13 suggested the current Boko Haram violence is in protest over Westernized culture and education which the Igbos represent. The Northerners were given the favor to maintain their traditional policies and religion during the colonial era and participants' suggestions indicate they still detest Westernized ways of doing things. The 63-year-old participant stated that although they are not strangers to these so called Western-influenced behaviors like drinking alcohol, prostitution, nudity, education, etc., they would rather prefer it done in secret than publicly.

Stepaniants (n.d.) also noted that loyalties to European-imposed identities are based on common characteristics of language, custom, religion, race, and territory that bind the community together (p. 5). The Hausa-Fulanis in the North were carved out from the upper Niger basin that comprises Mali, Niger, and Chad Republic (Ejiogu, 2013, p. 658). Islamic religion was introduced to them by the Sarakis when they were conquered in a Jihadist war before their experiences with the colonial masters. The Northerners still have connections with the upper Niger Basin countries where they were carved out from. Most participants in the interview suggested people from the neighboring countries of Northern Nigeria instigated or fueled most of the violence. Participant 24 stated how violence broke out on their border market days. They usually engaged in border trading on Tuesdays and Thursdays at Yobe border (Adamawa state capital) with neighboring countries of Niger, Chad, and Mali. Violence broke out in the midst of their transactions with bomb explosions. In the midst of the violence, he observed airstrikes and gunshots from armored military trucks that made it difficult for him to understand if it was the Nigeria military government trying to fight back or the insurgents. However, he stated the killings targeted young Igbo men while the women were captured and raped openly.

Participants 4 and 13 suggested most of the top military officers in Nigeria are indigenes of neighboring countries that nationalized in Nigeria. They believe some retired military officers in the North are instigators of the Boko Haram crisis in order to advance their political goals and further the possibility of Islamizing Nigeria. Participant 13 stated he knows most of the officials involved in the Boko Haram violence and mentioned the former and current presidential candidate Muhammad Buhari to be one of them.

Ethnicity/Social Class

Ethnicity may overlap with social class or status in deeply divided societies "where structures of discrimination block social mobility of specific groups" (Bangura, 1994, p. 9). In Nigeria, complaints of Northern dominance of federal power and inequality in distribution of infrastructure prompted the Eastern secession plan that preceded the Biafran War. The then Eastern governor Gen. Ojukwu stated the Northern allegation that the Igbos were responsible for the 1966 coup was due to their long despise for Igbos' success in trade and commerce across the nation. Virtually all participants stated the Igbos were targets of the violence because they were successful in business, and owned major investments and building structures in the North. Participants 3, 11, and 15 stated the Igbos are continually discriminated against in accessing jobs, education, and justice in the North. Participant 11 narrated how he would not bother taking any Hausa/Fulani to court because cases involving them and the Igbos are usually ignored. Participant 15 lamented on how she is tired of being disrespected on the streets by the beggars (almagiris) and how women who do not cover-up in veils are assaulted and raped on the streets of major Northern Nigeria without any intervention from the authorities. According to her, non-indigenes are always scared to do anything as any move can instigate violence. Participant 13 talked about the beheading of an Igbo man that was alleged to have cleaned up his bottom with a page of the Koran after using the toilet. Although the case was in court, the man was attacked on the streets and beheaded. Nothing was done by the authorities even after the Igbos protested openly. Participant 3 concluded by stating there are two classes of people in the Northern Nigeria: the privileged Hausa-Muslim who can do anything and get away with it and the marginalized Igbo-Christian who gets into trouble for saying or doing anything.

Psychological Factors of Deprivation

Psychologists suggest that people who do not benefit from development face a crisis of identity (Bangura, 1994, p. 24). They were found to face such crisis "when they are uprooted from traditional life or find it difficult to satisfy their ambitions when confronted with the pressures of modernity" (p. 24). Relative deprivation, which generates feelings of frustrations and a desire to express them in aggressive ways, was found to influence ethnic violence (p. 24). This ideology could be applicable to majority of Hausa-Islamic Northerners because of their lack of ambition in life and dislike for Western education. Generally, Hausa-Fulanis are known to lag behind in education and wealth when compared to other regions. They believe in loyalty and service to their religious leaders as means of obtaining daily meals and economic survival. The United Nations Research Institute for Social Development states instigators of ethnic violence compete for loyalties of their followers because of other relationships or commitment to others that blind them from the consequences of their action (Bangura, 1994, p. 4). Their loyalty to the religious community leaders and grievance as non-beneficiaries of societal development make them accessible instruments for political aims of the elites.

The alamagiris are usually toddlers that were kicked out of their homes to live with the "Imams" to study the Quaran (Islamic religion). They usually transition to selling Kola-nuts (mee kworo), shoe shiners, or candy sellers/currency exchangers. Their general ideology is to live for today and allow Allah (God) to take care of tomorrow (future). Others would rather sit around the Alhajis and Hajias (wealthy Muslims that have traveled to Mecca—Islamic holy land) to run errands. Part of their routine is to be on the streets in the evenings to beg for alms from the Alhajis/Hajia.

These Alhajis or retired military Hausa/Fulanis depend on government contracts based on their connections with the officials for economic benefits and livelihood. The almagiris and their adult counterparts on the streets are suggested to be behind numerous episodes of violence that occur in Northern Nigeria. Majority of the violence erupt as they are coming out of the mosques for their weekly Friday prayers. Religion is usually used in justifying the purposes of violence.

On the other hand, a striking characteristic of the traditional Igbo people is the absence of centralized authority. This sense of autonomy is visible in their popular associated proverb: "Igbo enweghi eze" (the Igbos have no kings or chiefs). The pro-colonized Igbo people practiced a participatory administrative system that allows the people to make decisions based on most popular consent based on experience and knowledge (Iro, 2014). The Igbos are mostly academicians and traders. They are referred to as the apostles of Nigeria because of their ability to travel the globe far and wide for trade and business purposes. An Igbo man would rather die trying to make it in life than stay poor. Their respect for one another is based on achievements rather than wealth or placements in society. Titles are gained based on philanthropic works done in society.

An Igbo man quickly transitions from apprenticeship to owner of a small business. Their mentors usually settle them with some amount of money or small portion of the store after they successfully complete their service term. They grow their business quickly because of their learned knowledge and experience gained during the apprentice period. They become the envies of the Northerners because they watched their progress from the apprentice period to owners of businesses and chains of investments. This is visible in the views of the 98 percent of participants that suggested the Igbos are targets of Northern Nigeria violence due to their wealth and investments in the North. Participant 5 pleaded for a bridge in the education gap between the Hausas and Igbos and eradication of alamagiris as a solution to the recurring violence in the North.

Political purpose was another reason that spread amongst participants' accounts for recurring violence in the North. Although "ethnic differences do not always translate into open violence", it can, however, "lead to violence, create widespread instability and loss of life" where there are political mobilizers or organizations that activate them (Bangura, 1994, p. 9). Politically, the primordial nature of ethnicity makes the people "favor members of their own groups where they had a choice between them and outsiders" (p. 5). Those that cited ethnic and political reasons for the violence suggested they are intended to frustrate the current President and hinder the Igbos from ascending to the presidential level of the government. Participants narrated their experiences during the 1993 M. K. O. Abiola's and 2011 Goodluck Jonathan's presidential election violence. Participant 6 narrated how an entire compound and its surroundings housing Igbo people were set on fire at night because they were known to have voted for the current Nigerian president and celebrated openly at the announcement of the result. Participants 12, 21, 22, and 28 suggested the violence mostly occurred in APC (All Progressives Party) Northern affiliated cities that include Bornu, Yobe, Nassarawa, Kano, and Zamfara states. To them, its purpose is to eliminate the Igbos in those cities for a possible win in the Presidential elections as they will likely vote against their candidates.

Summary of Stated Causal Factors

Common phrases as causal factor for violence amongst participants included: non-indigenes/Christians, jealousy of Igbo's business progress, dislike for education and Western values by the insurgents, unacceptance of Igbos in the North, and violence as tactic to scare and minimize Igbos' votes in the North for continual election win at the federal level. These views lined up with Chinua Achebe's perceptions of the reasons for pre-Biafran War violence. Participants also indicated that the violence is initiated or supported by neighboring Northern Nigerian countries from the upper Niger/Saharan regions like Chad, Niger, and Mali where the Hausa/Fulanis were carved from by the colonial government. Solidarity for common religious belief and need for Islamizing Nigeria were major reasons given by participants. The Igbo victims stated they fled back to their Eastern region through the Cameroonian borders, the historical background of the Igbos. Overall, wealth disparity, religious/cultural differences, and power struggles dominated participants' reasons why Igbos are targeted in Northern Nigerian violence. Nineteen of the participants interviewed experienced violence while living in Northern APC political affiliated states suggesting intentions of political dominance of federal power.

Tables 6–11 and Table 12 are a compilation of major Nigerian federal cabinet officials in regions and religious groups. Participants' interviews indicate violence episodes were intended to stop Igbos from voting for their regional candidates while living in the North. Participants also indicated they were told the Hausa-Fulani are meant to rule the country. Ethnicity and religion were interchangeably used to explain reasons why they were victims of violence.

Major federal government cabinets, military colleges, and unit dispositions were analyzed in ethnic and religious groups to seek similarities in office holders with participants' perception that they are discriminated in federal jobs. The demographic disposition of the country indicates the three major regions are dominated by a particular religion. Analysis of the officers demonstrates religious inclination based on region of origin.

Violence as Tactics for Domination of Federal Power

Colonial regionalization and ethnicization of political parties influenced competition amongst the three major regions. Adoption of the Hausa-Fulani political system and incorporation of their elites in the colonial administration gave them the impression they were meant to rule the country. Colonial masters favored them in distribution of infrastructure and lowered the quota for entrance into the military. The standard for admission into the military colleges was "lowered to favor the Northerners" making them have absolute majority in the Nigeria Army (Atorfarti, 1992). Violence against the Igbos in the North began as far back as 1957 when the former held a rally protesting over the amalgamation of the North and South. Prior to the Biafran War, there were no military units within the entire mid-western regions of Nigeria (Atorfarti, 1992, p. 8). Only one infant brigade was located in Enugu, the then eastern regional headquarters and an administrative office for logistics purposes in the southern part of Lagos. Atofarati reports the concentration of military units and dominance of military sectors placed the Northerners at an advantage during the Biafran War. As Bacik (2002) noted, violence can emanate amongst ethnic groups to retain their benefits or for fear of losing them (p. 20). The Biafran War was fought by the Hausa dominated federal government against the Igbos.

Federal Government Cabinet Leaders in Regions and Religious Groups

Tables 6–11 are an analysis of major Nigerian Federal Government Cabinets to determine domination of federal power by the North as informed in the literature review and through participants' perceptions. Participants suggested the 1993 Abiola and 2011 Jonathan Presidential violence were intended for Northerner's win of elections in the North and dominance of federal power. Others stated such violence usually occurs in Northern affiliated APC (All Progressive Congress party) cities in the North.

Nigerian Heads of Staff/Presidents, Ministers of Defense, Chief of Army Staff, Central Bank of Nigeria officials, and Army Unit locations were selected for the federal government cabinet analysis because they represent "the main stronghold for security, and defense of the country" (Oduyela, 2013, p. 1). The armored, infantry, and artillery corps are the main arms of the Nigerian Army with the mission of defending and protecting the national interest of the country. The Nigeria Army was established in 1979 to formulate and execute policies and programs towards attaining national security (Nigerian Army, 2014). The Chief of Army Staff reports to the Defense Minister—the highest ranking military officer in the army.

Table 6

Presidents/Heads of State from 1960 Independence Year to 2014 in Regions/Ethnic Groups

Name	Term/Reign	Duration	State of origin	Ethnicity	Religion	Comment
Nnamdi Azikiwe (Governor-General First President)	10/1/1960 – 1/15/1966	2 years 107 days	Anambra	Igbo	Christian	Over thrown
Sir Abubakar Tafawa Balewa (Prime Minister)	10/1/1960 – 1/15/1966	6 years 14 days	Bauchi	Hausa/Fulani	Muslim	Assassinated
Major Aguyi-Ironsi	01/16/1966 – 07/12/1966	177 days	Abia	Igbo	Christian	Over thrown
Gen. Yakubu Gowon	08/01/1966 – 01/29/1975	8 years 362 days	Plateau	Hausa/Fulani	Christian	Over thrown
Gen. Murtala Mohammed	07/29/1975 – 02/13/1976	199 days	Kano	Hausa/Fulani	Muslim	Assassinated
Major Gen. Olusegun Obasanjo	02/13/1976 – 10/01/1978	3 years/258 days	Ogun	Yoruba	Christian	Resigned
Shehu Shagari	10/01/1979 – 12/31/1983	4 years 91 days	Sokoto	Hausa/Fulani	Muslim	Over thrown
Muhammadu Buhari	12/31/1983 – 08/27/1985	1 year/239 days	Katsina	Hausa/Fulani	Muslim	Over thrown
Gen. Ibrahim Babangida	08/27/1985 – 08/26/1993	7 years/364 days	Niger	Hausa/Fulani	Muslim	Resigned
Ernest Shonekan	08/27/1993 – 11/17/1993	83 days	Ogun	Yoruba	Christian	President Interim Government
Gen. Sani Abacha	11/17/1993 – 06/08/1998	4 years/203 days	Kano	Hausa/Fulani	Muslim	Died in office
Gen. Abdulsalami Abubakar	06/08/1998 – 05/29/1999	355 days	Niger	Hausa/Fulani	Muslim	Resigned Transferred to civilian
Olusegun Obasanjo	05/29/1999 – 05/29/2007	8 years	Ogun	Yoruba	Christian	civilian government
Umaru Musa Yar'Adua	05/29/2007 – 05/05/2010	2 years, 341 days	Katsina	Hausa, Fulani	Muslim	Died in office
Goodluck Jonathan	05/05/2010 – Current	4 years 144 days	Bayalsa	Eastern Region	Christian	Interim to current

Source: Nigerian military almanac 2014/biographic pages (Nigerian Army, 2014).

Table 7

Ministers of Defense from 1975-2014

Alh. Muhammadu Ribadu	'60s	Unspecified	Adamawa	Hausa-Fulani	Muslim	Records of his years in the office was unavailable
Illiya Bisalla	1975-1976	1 year	Adamawa	Hausa-Fulani	Muslim	
Iya Abubakar	1979-1981	2 years	Adamawa	Hausa-Fulani	Muslim	
Akanbi Oniyangi	1981 to 1983	2 years	Kwara	Yoruba	Muslim	
Domkat Bali	1984 to 1990	6 years	Plateau	Hausa-Fulani	Muslim	
Sani Abacha	1990-1994	4 years	Kano	Hausa-Fulani	Muslim	
Theophilus Danjuma	1999-2003	3 years	Taraba	Hausa-Fulani	Christian	
Rabiu Kwankwaso	2003-2007	4 years	Kano	Hausa-Fulani	Muslim	
Thomas I. Aguyi-Ironsi	2006-2007	1 year	Abia	Igbo	Christian	
Yayale Ahmed	2007-2008	1 year	Bauchi	Hausa-Fulani	Muslim	
Shettima Mustapha	2008-2009	1 year	Yobe	Hausa-Fulani	Muslim	
Godwin Abbe	2009-2010	2 years	Edo	Yoruba	Christian	
Adetokunbo Kayode	2010-2011	1 year	Ondo	Yoruba	Muslim	
Dr. Bello Haliru Mohammed	07/2011-06/2012	1 year	Kebbi	Hausa-Fulani	Muslim	
Dr. Erelu Olusola Obada	07/2012-09/2013	1 year	Osun	Yoruba	Christian	
Gen. Aliyu Gusau	03/2014-current	1 year	Zamfara	Hausa-Fulani	Muslim	

Source: *Teniola (2014)*.

Table 8

Chiefs of Army Staff from 1963-2014

Name	Period	Duration	State of Origin	Ethnicity	Comments
Maj Gen. CB Welby-Everard OBE, KBE	1963-1965	2 Years	-	British	Last British Officer of the Nigerian Army
Maj Gen. JTU Aguiyi-Ironsi GCON MVO MBE	2/9/1965-1/16/1966	1 year/1 mo	Abia	Igbo	
Gen. Y. Gowon FSS	1/1966 - 7/1966	6 months	Plateau	Hausa/Fulani	
Col. JRI Akahan OFR FSS	5/1966 - 5/1968	2 Years	Benue	Middle Belt	
Maj Gen. Hu Katsina OFR, FSS, psc	5/1968 - 1/1971	3 years	Katsina	Hausa/Fulani	
Maj. Gen DA Ejoor DSM GSM NSM psc	1/1971 - 7/1975	4 years/6mo	Edo	Yoruba	
Lt. Gen TY Danjuma GCON FSS psc	7/1975-10/1979	4 years/3mo	Taraba	Hausa/Fulani	
Lt. Gen IA Akinrinade CFR FSS	10/1979-1980	1 year	Osun	Yoruba	
Gen GS Jallo OFR FSS JSSC	4/1980-10/1981	1 year/6 mo	Adamawa	Hausa/Fulani	
LT Gen MI Wushishi CFR FSS psc Usawc	10/1981-12/1983	2 years/2 mo	Adamawa	Hausa/Fulani	
Maj Gen Ibrahim Badamasi Babangida GCFR DSS psc mni	1/1984-8/1985	1 year/7mo	Minna	Hausa/Fulani	
Gen S. Abacha GCON DSS psc mni	08/1985-09/1990	6 years/1 mo	Kano	Hausa/Fulani	
Lt Gen S. Ibrahim	08/1990 - 09/1993	3 years/1 mo	Kano	Hausa/Fulani	
Lt Gen A. Mohammed DSS psc rcds	09/1993 - 11/1993	2 months	Zamfara	Hausa/Fulani	
Maj Gen Mohammed Chris Alli CRG DSS ndc psc (+)	11/1993-03/1994	9 months	Plateau	Hausa/Fulani	
Maj Gen AJ Kazir DSS psc (+) Usawc	08/1994-03/1996	1 year/7mo	Yobe	Hausa/Fulani	
Lt Gen IR Bamaiyi GCON mni psc (+)	3/1996-5/1999	3 years/2mo	Kebbi	Hausa/Fulani	
Lt Gen SVL Malu mni, fwc DSO DSS psc	5/1999-2001	2 years	Benue	Tiv	
Lt Gen AO Ogomudia CRR DSS fwc psc(+) Msc FNSE	4/2001-06/2003	2 years/2 mo	Delta	Mid-West	
Lt Gen ML Agwai CFR GSS psc (+) fwc	6/2003 - 6/2006	3 years	Kaduna	Hausa/Fulani	
Lt Gen Owoye Andrew Azizi CFR DSS GSS psc (+) fwc	6/2006-6/2007	1 year	Bayelsa	Niger Delta	
Lt Gen Luka Nyeh Yusuf CFR GSS GPP DSO psc(+) fwc	6/2007-8/2008	1 year/2 mo	Kaduna	Hausa/Fulani	
Lt Gen AB Dambazau CFR GSS psc ndc fwc(+) PhD FNIPR	08/2008-09/2010	2 years/1mo	Niger	Hausa/Fulani	
Lt Gen OA Ihejirika CFR GSS psc(+) fwc fniqs	09/2010 -1/2014	3 years/8 mo	Abia	Igbo	
Lt Gen KTJ Minimah CMH GSS psc (+) fwc MSc	Current	Current	Bayelsa	Eastern region	

Source: *Nigerian Army (2014).*

Table 9

Chief Justices of Nigeria from 1958-2012

Chief Justice	Term	Duration	State of Origin	Ethnicity/Region	Comments
Hon. Justice Ademola Adetokumbo, KBE, CON	1958–1972	14 years	Abeokuta	Yoruba	
Hon. Justice Tashim Olawale Elias, CFR, GCON	1972–1975	3 years	Lagos	Yoruba	
Hon. Justice Darley Arthur Alexander	1975–1979	4 years	N/A	St Lucia, British West Indies	Non-Nigerian
Hon. Justice Atanda Fatai William, CON	1979–1983	4 years	Lagos	Yoruba	
Hon. Justice George Sodeinde Womemimo, CON, GCON	1983–1985	2 years	Ogun	Yoruba	
Hon. Justice Ayo Gabriel Irikefe, OFR, CON, GCON	1985–1987	2 years	Lagos	Yoruba	
Hon. Justice Mohammed Bello, CON, GCON	1987–1995	8 years	Katsina	Hausa/Fulani	
Hon. Justice Muhammad Lawal Uwais, CON, GCON	1995–2006	11 years	Kaduna	Hausa/Fulani	
Hon. Justice Salihu Moddibo Alfa Belgore, CON, GCON	2006–2007	1 year	Kwara	Yoruba	
Hon. Justice I. L. Kutigi	2007–2009	2 years	Niger	Hausa/Fulani	
Hon. Justice Aloysius Iyorgyer Katsina-Alu	2009–2011	2 years	Benue	Middle Belt	
Hon. Justice Dahiru Mustapha	2011–2012	1 year	Jigawa	Hausa/Fulani	
Hon. Justice Aloma Mariam Mukhtar	2012– incumbent	Current	Kano	Hausa/Fulani	

Source: Federal Judicial Service Commission (2015).

114

Table 10

CBN Governors from 1958 to 2014

CBN Governors	Term	Duration	Ethnicity/Region	State of Origin	Religion
Roy Pentelow Fenton	07/24/1958-7/24/1963	5 years	N/A	British	N/A
Alh. Aliyu Mai-Bornu	07/25/1963-6/22/1967	4 years	Bornu	Hausa/Fulani	Muslim
Dr. Clement Nyong Isong	8/15/1972-9/24/1975	3 years 34days	Cross River	Eastern	Christian
Mal. Adamu Ciroma	9/24/1975-6/28/1977	1 yr 94 days	Yobe	Hausa/Fulani	Muslim
Mr. O. O. Vincent	6/28/1977-6/28/1982	5 years	Lagos	Yoruba	Christian
Alh. Abdulkadir Ahmed	6/28/1982-9/30/1993	11 yrs. 92 days	Bauchi	Hausa/Fulani	Muslim
Dr. Paul A. Ogwuma, OFR	10/1/1993-5/29/1999	5 yrs	Abia	Igbo	Christian
Chief (Dr.) J. O. Sanusi, CON	5/29/1999-5/29/2004	5 yrs	Ondo	Mid-Western	Christian
Prof Chukwuma C. Soludo, CFR	5/29/2004-5.28.2009	5 yrs	Anambra	Igbo	Christian
Mal. Sanusi Lamido Sanusi	6/4/2009-05/30/2014	5 yrs	Kano	Hausa/Fulani	Muslim
Mr. Godwin Emefiele	6/2/2014-Current	Current	Delta	Mid-Western	Christian

Source: Central Bank of Nigeria (n.d.) – Past and Present Governors

Table 11

Nigeria Military Colleges/Units

S/N	Military/Airforce Commands	Location	State	Region	Comments
1	Nigeria Defence Academy	Zaria	Kaduna	Northern	
2	National Defence College (Formerly National War College)	Abuja	Abuja	Northern	
3	Armoured School	Bauchi	Bauchi	Northern	
4	School of Infantry	Jaji	Kaduna	Northern	
5	Airforce Training School	Zaria	Kaduna	Northern	
6	Armed Forces Command/staff College (mid-riff training center)	Jaji	Kaduna	Northern	
7	School of Artillery	Kotongora	Niger	Northern	
8	Depot of Nigerian Army (Training Infantry)	Zaria	Kaduna	Northern	
9	Training/Doctrine Command (TRADOC)	Minna	Niger	Northern	Training/Combat development with R&D outfit.
9	1 Mechanized Division HQ	Kaduna	Kaduna	Northern	Established during the war to secure Area of Operation (AOP)
10	2 Mechanized Division HQ	Ibadan	Oyo	Southern	Established during the war to secure Area of Operation (AOP)
11	3 Armoured Division HQ	Jos	Plateau	Northern	Established during the war to secure Area of Operation (AOP0
12	7th Infantry Division	Kaduna	Kaduna	Northern	Established in 2013 in addition to 23 Brigade in Yola (Adamawa) 21 Brigade in Maiduguri (both in the North) and 22 Brigade in Ilorin (Southern).
13	81 Division – (Lagos Garrison Command)	Ikeja	Lagos	Southern	Upgraded from 4 Infantry Division with two battalions (165/19 Mechanized Battalions) to provide security in Lagos and parts of Ogun State.
14	82 Composite Division HQ	Enugu	Enugu	Eastern	Established in 1975 with securing its Area of Responsibility (AOR) of South/Eastern and South/Southern Flanks
15	83rd Mechanized Division	Benin City	Niger Delta	Mid-Western	Formed in 2001/02; does not appear in Nigerian Army website but has Orbat.com Identification.

Source: Global Security (2014).

Table 12

Summary of the Major Federal Appointments by Regions from 1957-2015

Regions	Heads of State/Presidents	Defense Ministers	Chief of Army Staff	Chief of Justices	CBN Governors
Hausa/Fulani	37 years/9days	24 years	34 years/2months	25 years	21 years/186 days
Yoruba	11years/342 days	6 years	1 year	25 years	10 years
Igbo	2 years/284 days	1 year	4 years/9 months	-	10 years
Others	4 years/144 days	-	14 years/8 months	3 years	3 years/34 days

Regional analyses of the officials indicate no Igbo ethnic group had been appointed head of State or Nigerian President, Chief of Army Staff, or Minister of Justice since after the 1966/67 military coups. Available records indicate that no Igbo had occupied these positions since after 40 years of independence and 30 years after the Biafran War (Onwuka, 2014). The first Igbo Defense Minister since 1966 was appointed in 2007, and the tenure lasted for only one year. In 2010, the current President "Goodluck Jonathan replaced the Heads of Army, Navy and Airforce due to militant Boko Haram insurgency" (Global Security, 2014). Lt. Gen. O. A. Ihejirika and Gen. K. T. J Minimah from Abia and Bayelsa states were appointed Chief of Army staff from 2010 to the present. The Yorubas enjoyed two tenures and an interim government with Obansanjo as the only candidate in the military and democratic president.

Nigerian Presidency/Heads of State, the Defense Ministers, and Chief of Army Staff have been dominated by the Hausa/Fulanis. They ruled the country as either head of state or president for 37 years out of its 54 years since independence: twenty-four years as dominant Ministers of Defense and 34 years as Chief of Army Staff respectively. These officers helped in the expansion and the domination of military installation and units in the North (Teniola, 2014). The state capital was moved from Lagos to Abuja under the office of Ibrahim Bagangida in 1979; no other ethnic group has been appointed Minister of the Abuja Federal Capital. The position has been dominated by the Hausa/Fulani ethnic group. Other regions of the country have a combined total of about 18 years ruling the country with two years apportioned to the Igbo ethnic group. The Yorubas had a total of about 12 years through Major General Obansanjo who ruled as Military Head of State and Civil President.

Nigeria continues to witness the intervention of the army from the Defense Ministers and Army Chiefs in its governance. Gen. Yakubu Gowon, Ibrahim Babangida, and Sanni Abacha assumed the Head of State through coup-d'état. Some of the retired military came back, vied, and ruled as presidents under the democratic elections. These Generals also had longevity records in the their rulings; Obansanjo

117

had a combined total of 11 years as a Head of State and President, Yakubu Gowon ruled for eight years plus, while Ibrahim Babangida stayed in the office for seven years and 364 days (one day from eight years). Gen. Muhammed Buhari at his 76th birthday and having ruled the country for almost eight years is currently vying for the 2015 presidential election. The international *New York Times* of January 23, 2015 reports the General is being looked up to as the solution to the current prevailing Boko Haram violence in most Northern Nigerian cities (Nossiter, 2015). Local reports, however, suggest he is the brain behind the insurgents as a means of frustrating the current president and advancing himself to the office.

Like its other significant sectors, the CBN and its governors control the operations and economic policies of the country. Its objective is to ensure monetary/price stability, maintain external reserves, and provide economic and financial advice to the government (Central Bank of Nigeria, n.d.). Central Bank governors' positions have favored the Igbos with a combined total of ten years out of the country's 54 years of independence. The Yorubas and Hausas dominated the office of Justice Ministers with 25 years respectively out of a total of 54 years. No Igbo ethnic group has been found worthy of the post since 1953 to date of writing.

About 90 percent of Nigerian Army School and units are also located within the Northern Region. Other units such as the logistics, administrative, and ceremonial units are installed in Lagos, Enugu, and other mid-western regions of the state. World Global Security reports the establishment of 13 Amphibious Brigade in 2010 that was not attested in 1999.

Domination of Federal Power - A Northern Birth-Right

The British colonial government favored the Northerners with political power and infrastructure allocations by adopting the Northern political system and incorporating their elites into their government. Dominance of federal power, military units, and top officials continues to place the Northerners at an advantage in perpetuating violence and injustice on the Igbo ethnic group. The literature review notes that during the 1967 coup, the Igbo military and civilians were sought from their homes and places of business and executed in their thousands. During the Biafran War, Atofarati (1992) states there was only one military unit in the whole of the Eastern region making it impossible for the Igbos to defend themselves (p. 8). The war was fought in residential areas of the Igbos. Children, the elderly, and pregnant women were killed and raped indiscriminately. Recurring violence after the Biafran War have taken the same trend. Bombings, killings, and burning of houses, stores, and churches are concentrated within the Igbo residential areas at Sabon-Gari quarters, places of worship, and other gatherings. Participants recounted how entire sections of the cities where Igbos reside were leveled out with bomb explosions. People are sorted individually from their houses and executed before their families. Others are sent personal letters or text messages asking them to leave the North or face being killed. Women without veils are abused and raped openly by the alamajiris.

An intriguing occurrence with majority of the violence is that access to communication is disrupted prior to and during the times of violence making it impossible for victims to reach their loved ones. Those who are able to escape from the city end up running to the military barracks for protection. However, despite the numerous military infantry and brigade units with its top officials in the North, they are unable to combat the violence or maintain peace in the North. Most interviewees wondered why the Nigerian Military that had assisted other African countries such as Sierra Leon and ECOMOG in winning their battles are unable to handle Boko Haram and other crisis in the North.

Since the history of the nation, no Igbo has assumed the position of Defense Minister and Chief of Army Staff prior to Jonathan's regime from the table of analysis. The first Easterner assigned the Chief of Army staff was in 2010 by the current president Goodluck Jonathan. The federal Northern-dominated Heads of States/Presidents continued to appoint their Hausa/Fulani brothers to these sensitive security positions for continuous domination and marginalization of the Igbos.

Alhaji Galadima in defense for the credibility of former Defense Minister Gen. Aliyu Gasau states the minister helped recruit almost all the famous Heads of State and Army Staff. The Generals particularly from Niger State of the Northern region include General Ibrahim Babangida, Gado Nasko, Abdulsalam Abubakar, Mamman Vasta, Sanni Abacha, and the appointment of Inua Wada (uncle to former Head of State, Gen. Murtala Muhammed) as Defense Minister (Teniola, 2012). These Generals were the bedrock of the military that championed major bloody coups in the country.

Based on report analysis and participants' interviews, the military continually takes sides with the Hausa/Fulanis in most Northern violence. Participant 24 stated how he noticed military armored trucks in the violence that broke out at the border trade in Yobe State. He stated there were airstrikes within the non-indigenous quarters where the Igbos reside, leveling an entire section of the city. Global Security (2014) alleged a possible sabotage of Nigerian military in handling the Boko Haram issue stating the junior officers would rather face court martial than obey the orders of its corrupt leaders. Nigerian military continued to flee from Boko Haram insurgents or allegedly lost their military weapons to them. Participant 13, a 63-year-old man, suggested he knew Northern political elites instigating the Boko Haram insurgents and relocated for fear of them killing him because of his inside knowledge.

In a clash involving Fulani herdsmen in Benue, the military were witnessed in the killing of civilians and destruction of their properties. Local newspapers reported on how the 3rd Division of the Yola Brigade killed over 200 unarmed civilians and destroyed shops, public buildings, and properties in Benue state (Ciboh, 2014; Human Rights Watch, 2002). In a similar occurrence, the soldiers took sides with Fulani herdsmen in a killing of Tiv farmers. Domination of Nigeria military colleges and military units in the North put the non-indigenous settlers at risk. They continually flee back to their region for fear of being extradited based on past experiences of the 1967 coup and Biafran War.

Fight for National Cake: Officials Corruption/Misappropriation of Public Funds

Continuous dominance of Hausa/Fulani in federal power has assured better provisions of basic amenities of life such as good roads, electricity, and public health to the Northerners. These provisions have been the major attraction for foreign indigenous immigrants to the region since the colonial era. Interviewees stated how they have been unable to cope financially since relocating back to the East and looked forward to moving back. Participant 8 compared the segregation of Kaduna into the North and South to what is going on in the entire country.

Embezzlement of public funds by government officials is leveraged for personal and political gains. This practice helps keep the alamagiris and other insurgent payrolls for continual disruption of peace and killings in the North. The 63-year-old participant accused the former Head of State Muhammadu Buhari of being behind the ongoing Boko Haram insurgence and former governor Ali Sherrif of using violence to advance his political ambition for two tenures.

Ogbeidi (2012) discussed corruption amongst Nigerian leaders from the pre-colonial era and notes leaders were known to pay more attention to their personal and ethnic groups than they did to the issues of the general public (p. 6). Leaders from both the military and democratic eras were involved and practiced behaviors that "provided fertile ground for corruption at all sectors" (p. 8). Mismanagement, bribery, and misuse of public funds for personal gains have become a cultural phenomenon for the country and its government officials. Reports of the investigations from the first republic government revealed that government officials registered and awarded contracts to their private businesses from major public parastatals like the Nigeria Railway Corporation, Nigerian Ports Authority, Nigerian Airways, and the then Electric Corporations of Nigeria.

Dr. Nnamdi Azikiwe, the first Republican President, obtained bank loans of over 163,000 pounds from the then African

Continental Bank where he was a principal stakeholder (Ogbeidi, 2012, p. 8). The Foster-Sutton Tribunal suggested the leader was guilty of not relinquishing his involvement in private business according to the pubic office code of conduct. Chief Obafemi Awolowo under the Coker Commission of inquiry was found guilty of a similar offense. The National Investment and Properties Co. Ltd., Western Region Finance Corporation, and Western Nigeria Development Corporation received loans worth over 6.7 million pounds that were never repaid when he was part of the board of directors.

Gowon's government was found to have inflated a contract of 52 million Naira to 552 million in ordering for cement meant for the Ministry of Defense. The regime of Shehu Shagari was not left out as it marked the highest mismanagement of four billion Naira for rice importations by his Transport Minister, Umaru Dikko (Ogbeidi, 2012, p. 8). Federal government buildings were mysteriously burnt down at the commencement of the audit panel set to investigate the frauds. The Okigbo Panel that reported on Reorganization and Reformation of Central Bank of Nigeria indicated Gen. Ibrahim Babangida, Gen. Sani Abacha, and the former CBN governor Alh. Abdulkadir Ahmed conspired with other top official in misappropriating about "$12.4 billion oil windfall between 1988 and 1994" (p. 9). Gen. Ibrahim Babangida's thirteen year regime witnessed alarming indiscriminate corruption within the entire sectors of the country. General Ibrahim Babangida's regime officially opened the doors to corruption in all sectors when he pardoned all convicted officials and restored their ceased properties (Falana, 2015). While the former general could not account for the missing $12.4 billion during his regime, he however suggested he acquired his astonishing wealth from bank share investments and pensions alone. The general's enlisted wealth ranged from ownership of a private university to a 50 bedroom mansion in Minna. President Ibrahim Babangida was also accused of promoting officials that challenged his actions and put away others in jail without trial. People like Professor Tam David-West was jailed for six months for taking a gold wrist-watch gift from a foreign businessman while holding the office of a Petroleum Minister. The social critic stated the gesture was intended to humiliate him for "speaking out against the sleaze" he believed took place in the regime (Achebe, 2005, para. 4). Foreign journalist, William Keelings, was deported for writing on the president's "unprecedented looting of the treasury" (Falana, 2015, para. 34). A chief editor of *Newswatch* magazine, Dele Giwa, was killed by a time bomb while having breakfast with his family (Falana, 2015, para. 4). The journalist had reported on the general's wife's association in drug businesses and had refused an offer for monetary settlement as an alternative.

A *Justice News* report stated that Sani Abacha hid over $458 million in foreign accounts (United States Department of Justice, 2014). The U.S. Department of Justice later authorized the funds to be frozen after an FBI report. Three hundred and thirteen million dollars and $145 million were found in his private accounts in Bailiwick of Jersey, France, and United Kingdom respectively (U.S. Department of Justice, 2014, para. 2). Abacha adopted high-leveled autocratic, pro-human-rights policies to further Hausa/Fulani ethnic and personal intentions. Abacha's government banned all political parties, removed all civilians from his cabinets, dissolved all labor unions, and jailed opposing opponents ("Nigeria," 2007). During his tenure King Saro Wiwa and eight other Ogoni leaders protesting against continuous drilling of oil in their region were tried and executed within two weeks. Labor union leaders were indiscriminately jailed to stop them from challenging government policies or furthering their members' interest. MKO Abiola, the proposed winner of 1994 Presidential election, was jailed and later died in prison while his wife Kudirat Abiola was murdered following her protests (p. 10). Abacha's embezzlement and misappropriations topped any of its kind in the history of any African country.

Summary

Records of Heads of States indicate no Igbo ethnic group has ascended to the position of presidency since the 1966 military coup.

Gen. Aguiyi Ironsi accused of spear-heading the coup only graced the office for 177 days before he was forcefully removed. Hausa-Fulani Northerners have continually dominated the ruling of the country, followed by the Yorubas for 12 years through Obafemi Awolowo. The Northerners were also favored with greater access to military colleges, provision of necessary infrastructure, and being part of the ruling cabinet in the colonial government. These behaviors implanted the impression of the right to dominate other regions. After the European administration, Nigeria continually witnessed series of military coups from 1966 to 1998 that resulted to the establishment of a Northerner as Head of State or President.

In the democratic government, violence of different types continues to erupt in the North due to their fear of losing colonial benefits. Participants stated how their neighbors told them violence will end as soon as the current President Goodluck Jonathan steps down or the Igbos relinquish federal power to the North. They suggested ruling of the country was their right while the Igbos are meant to trade. Others stated how vehicle plate numbers had inscriptions of "born to rule" in the North.

Based on participants' assumptions of violence as tactics for political gain in the North and continuous domination of federal government power, five key federal cabinets' records and military dispositions were purposefully selected for analysis to find similarities in participants' perceptions and reviewed literature. Hausa/Fulani domination was found visible prior to independence to the year 2011.

Since majority of the officials investigated for embezzlement of public funds were mostly Northerners, it went a long way to support participants' views that the violence in the North is aimed at suppressing the Igbos from attaining federal government positions. Misappropriated monies as well as dominance of military officials and its units give Northern political elites leverage to finance violence and further their political aims for continuous dominance of the country's federal power.

Chapter 5

Summary of Study, Findings, and Recommendations

Three themes of Human Identity theory examine ethnic conflict. Primordalism assumes that ethnic groups are bounded through inherited natural occurrences that are rigid and stagnant. Accounts of violence suggest major regions of Nigeria are still tied to their primordial history. Pre-colonial historical countries like Niger, Chad, Mali, and Sudan influence the violence. Interview accounts suggest they pressure for the Islamization of major Northern states and that of the country. Their presence in top Nigerian military offices is believed to sabotage the efforts of resolving the conflicts in the North. The Igbos, on the other hand, find solace and escape to the Cameroons during violence suggesting existing ties with their pre-colonial lower Niger basin. Majority of participants recounted fleeing to Cameroons and finding peace before onward travels to the Eastern region of Nigeria. Instrumentalist relations acquired through social and political groups in Nigeria can be attributed to the ethnic discrimination in the country. Political parties and its membership are associated through regional and ethnic lines based on anticipated individual and ethnic benefit. Conflicts erupting in anger or protests over lost elections become ethnicized due to the regionalization of the political parties. Overall, colonial manipulations, regionalized administration, discrimination, and favoritism of the groups have continued to be the foundational reason for inter-ethnic conflict in major cities of Northern Nigeria. Manipulations of political parties and ethnicization of state bureaucracy are major causes. Segregation of ethnic groups in bureaucratic positions influences ethnic conflicts.

Participants' perceptions, journal reviews, and data analysis suggest that Northern Nigerian political elites use their strong religious group identity to incite violence for ethnic power and infrastructure distribution advantage. The creation of Sabon-Gari quarters for non-indigenous immigrants form concentration areas for violence and heightens casualties. Overall violence in major parts of Nigeria has been influenced by regionalized administration and ethnicization of political parties that have been built up since the colonial era.

Overall, numerous theories and scholastic views have been used to find connection to causes of Northern Nigeria violence as ethnically influenced. Data collection and analysis based on participants' perception of the violence were used in seeking similarities and understanding from the literature review, historical background, and interviews in drawing conclusions (Willis, 2007, p. 219; Yin, 1989, p. 13). Twenty-eight Igbo people from four locations that experienced the violence, and lost love ones or properties were interviewed to determine why they were victims of the violence.

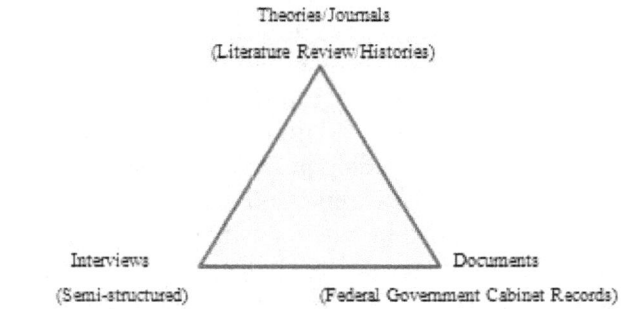

Figure 2. Model of data collection and analysis.

Findings

Based on interview analysis, more than 24 out of 28 participants found ethnic-related struggles in the violence. Participants' views and perspectives suggest the violence is based on Hausa-Muslim jealousy of Igbo-Christians' success in business and investments in the North.

Fear for loss of Northern self-identifications and colonial favors like religion, culture, and federal power dominance were found to agitate the violence. Hausa Islamic dislike for Western education and values that dates back to the colonial era represented in Igbos seems to threaten continual existence of Islamic values. Igbo-Christian women in Western dress/attire are harassed and abused to demonstrate that they do not belong and are not welcomed in the North.

Protecting colonial benefits of federal power dominance and major means of livelihood that depends on government allocations and contract jobs instigated political-related violence. Northern dominant Igbo-Christians that vote for their regional political parties are killed and scared away for possible win of the 12 Northern Nigeria states.

The Presidency, Nigerian Army Chiefs, Defense ministers, Ministers of Justice, and Central Bank governors that are essential in policymaking and economic distribution are kept away from the Igbos. The intention is to hinder them from ruling or progressing in a country they earlier seceded from. Domination of the military cabinets and its units by the North places them at advantage in times of conflict. The Igbos have continued to flee back to their regions for fear of extraditions experienced in 1967 coup and Biafran War.

Recommendations

Need for basic principles of democracy. When a country decides on democracy as its method of governance, instituting basic structures of democracy is essential to solidify the system and make it impossible for other alternative types of regime. Harris and Reilly (1998) suggest true consideration of democracy as a system of government is reached when there is complete institutionalization of democratic structures that "make alternative types of regime unthinkable" (p. 348). Society must believe that rising problems can be handled within the existing democratic structures and new sets of norms, laws, and institutions for dealing with conflicts should be incorporated in the structure.

Major principles of democracy as Harris and Reilly enumerated include transparency, accountability, and participation.

Accountability. Lack of accountability is a huge issue in the history of Nigeria. Accountability is the need for a government to be answerable to its people (Harris & Reilly, 1998, p. 350). However, the Nigerian government does not feel the need for accountability for their actions to the public. Ascending to government office is viewed as an instrument for power dominance, and suppression of the public towards misappropriation of public funds for ethnic and personal gains. The public are accountable to their government through respect for policies and submission to the authorities.

Politics and getting into government is seen as a means of sharing the national cake that has encouraged widespread corruption in all government sectors. Corruption is spread throughout all federal, state, and local government levels. It becomes difficult for the public to acquire basic services without offering bribes to the officials.

Bribery and corruption have become part of the cultural norm of Nigerian society from the janitor to the manager of any office. Government officials complain of no availability of supplies needed to do their jobs. Financial allocations for such supplies must have been redirected for other personal gains. The public, therefore, continually pay their way to obtain services that ordinarily should be provided freely by its government.

Doctors in public hospitals divert medical supplies and medications to their personal clinics and refer patients to them. At other times they might be made to buy the supplies that have already been provided by the government for public use. Bribery is openly practiced in all government offices and flows from the management to the entire staff. Lower level staff members collect the money and distribute them as appropriate to the management level. In offices like the Nigeria Immigration Services, codes such as "committed" are indicated on files of people that have paid additional requested money for their passports to signify the request can proceed.

Inability to settle or be accountable to the top officials puts the staff at risk for loss of job. For example, police officials on the street need to account for a certain amount of money to their supervisors on a daily or weekly basis to guarantee their jobs or placement at viable posts. Public offenses, especially by drivers, are meant to pay money instead of facing penalties for their offense. The money goes to the officer in charge who accounts to another officer or as a buy-over for mismanagement practices in the office.

General Ibrahim Babangida, the Nigerian head of state from 1985 to 1993, was accused of legalizing bribery and corruption in Nigeria. His government released all officials that were on trials for corruption, returned their ceased properties, and incorporated them into his government (Falana, 2015). Falana states his regime made it "common knowledge that official corruption was part of the directive principle of state policy" (para. 6). Irrespective of how the practices emanated or got justified, Nigeria is currently labeled as the most corrupt country in the world. The trend has made it impossible for provisions of basic living amenities like constant electricity, good roads, and public health to its citizens, yet Nigeria is the fifth largest world producer of oil.

Two major essentials of accountability are needed to monitor, review, and criticize government performance and separate judicial power (Harris & Reilly, 1998, p. 350). Legally separating judicial powers from all levels of government ensures checks and balances in government policies and behaviors of its officials.

Transparency. Transparency and accountability go hand in hand. Transparency "refers to the openness" of the operations of the government, and its systems to the public (Harris & Reilly, 1998, p. 349). It entails implementing policies that can be understood and scrutinized by the people. While participation in the area of public voting has been in existence in Nigeria, ensuring free and fair elections has been a struggle and the processes have continued to improve.

Acceptance of government elected officials through these fair elections has been of great challenge. Instituting democratic government is the acceptance that "alternative type of regime is unthinkable" (Harris & Reilly, 1998, p. 348). By operating processes and policies that are open helps build the trust, support, and cooperation necessary to sustain the government. Instituting checks and balances improves the responsibility and accountability of government and contributes to sustaining as well as legitimizing the processes (p. 349). Transparency helps eliminate secret policies aimed at marginalizing others for ethnic or personal purposes.

Participation. Participation is one area that needs great work in the Nigerian government system. Participation means sharing responsibilities in the government by the people in the system (Harris & Reilly, 1998, p. 351). It also entails participation of groups in society for the protection of their members' interest and that of the public. There is also the need for people to freely choose those they want to rule them without coercion of any sort. Although voting and ensuring free and fair elections is a crucial part of the concept, the need for ensuring participation of societal groups in the system is highly important.

Key agents of participation as Harris and Reilly (1998) enlisted includes incorporation of associations that are independent of the government and human rights organizations that reflect and advocate for the interests of the public (p. 351). Organizations like the press, trade unions, nongovernmental organizations, religious groups, professional organizations, etc., that represent the interests of their groups and the public should be allowed to operate freely in a democratic government.

Civil societies should be seen as intermediary units between the public and government that represent families, individuals, and groups which are a powerful part of the society (Harris & Reilly, 1998, p. 351). These groups as the authors suggest should be autonomous from government and allowed to operate, criticize, and act as check and balances for the accountability and transparency of the government (p. 351). Suppressing or opposing these groups as is regularly done by most in the Nigerian government regime "is a sign of weak and ineffective democratic government that endangers the interest of the public" (p. 351).

Steps towards Ensuring Proper Democratic Society

End of monopoly of government to a single state or political party. The beginning of a sustainable democratic government is ensuring a strong party system (Harris & Reilly, 1998, p. 351). Political parties should not be for state or regional ownership in which all citizens must vote in ethnic or regional lines. Projecting or anticipating a party that a state, ethnic, or region votes during elections demonstrates weakness in the party state. For example, Nigeria has continued to form parties and vote on regional and ethnic lines since the colonial era. Although much has changed in incorporating more parties, the three major regions continually dominate particular parties that signifies struggle for federal power domination. Violence occurs in Northern Nigeria in that regard when voting lines changed due to great increase of foreign indigenous immigrants to the region. Individuals are forced to vote for the dominant political party of the region or face being massacred. At other times, boxes of tomb-printed votes are moved to the region to rig the elections where regional voting turns against expectations.

In summation, incorporating the basic democratic principles of accountability, transparency, and participation in Nigeria will hinder struggle for dominance of power by any particular regional or political party that ignites violence and corruption. Separation of judicial power and non-suppression of participation of societal groups will hold government officials accountable, ensure checks

131

and balances, and minimize secret agendas that marginalize and hinder others from being accepted as full fledged members of the society.

For true democratic experience to take place in Nigeria, basic human rights need to be guaranteed and protected. Government officials need to face trials for mismanagement and misappropriation of public funds. By so doing, indiscriminate killings of people who oppose fictitious policies and mismanagement behaviors will be minimized. Proper accountability for government and its officials will help in sanitizing the Nigerian political system, minimize associated violence, and improve its entire economy. Attaining true democratic and accountable government is a process that might take more decades to achieve according to trends of the events in its 55 years of independence.

Strengths, Weaknesses, and Lesson Learned

This research makes a significant contribution to the school of Humanities and Social Sciences and Department of Conflict Analysis and Resolution. Several reports have been written in the past categorizing the Northern violence as socio-economic, religious, or politically related. This research in using identity theory tied contributing characteristics of Northern Nigerian violence to inter-ethnic unrest which is synonymous with other African countries that experienced British colonial administration. Ethnic groups are people who share common history, culture, religion, and language. These characteristics can influence violence when groups feel their identity is threatened. Extensive literature review on the background of major Nigerian regions and their experiences with European administration brings understanding on the external factors influencing the violence. This research perspective could help in mapping out better reconciliation strategies to the conflict that has lingered for over 40 years for possible peaceful co-existence of the groups in Northern Nigeria.

Certain limitations, however, exist for this study. Obtaining information from secondary sources could alter some data. However, these authors provided information that was not obtainable in Nigerian government official websites or archives necessary for the report. These authors' perspectives and the researcher's ethnicity as well as experiences of the violence could have impacted some interpretations. The Hausa or Islamic words and terminology may not have been appropriately spelled.

The sensitiveness and trend of events during the study could have also limited respondents. Some interviewees were afraid to share information due to uncertainty of the interviewer's identity and ongoing violence in the North. A larger sample population or study at a different time could produce different or more information that could have been relevant to the study.

Lessons Learned

A lot has been learned in the process of this study. Design of any good policy entails analysis of its short and long term effects before implementation. Contributory factors influencing Northern Nigerian violence emanates from government policies and practices as handed down by the European government that colonized the nation. Adopting Northern traditional ruling policies and incorporating Hausa/Fulani elites in the colonial government made the Northerners dependent on government provisions. It further instilled a feeling of the right to rule the country and fear of losing the power and associated benefits to other regions. Historical countries from which the major regions were carved still play significant roles in the conflict. While the Northern boundaries continue to instigate violence for possible Islamization of the country, Cameroon is a route for escape and solace for the Igbos during violence.

Discrimination in distribution of major infrastructures like military units and lowering of quotas in standards for admission to military colleges gave them security advantage used in subduing other regions for continual federal power dominance. The Igbo ethnic groups are yet to be accepted as part of the Nigeria Federation after their secession attempt that led to the 1967 Biafran War. The Northern Hausa-Fulani that fought in reuniting the nation have continually dominated and hindered the Igbos from ascending to positions of leadership and other sensitive posts in the military.

As a new researcher in this type of research field, the sensitiveness of the study and possible obstacles were under-estimated. However, the study provided great opportunity in researching a real life issue that is personal to the researcher.

Areas for Further Study

This study associated the violence as ethnically related using the human identity theory. The theory did not address how ethnic peace can be achieved. Further studies could be conducted on the impact of the variables on the violence and how peace can be achieved. Since much work has been done on religious and colonial contributions to the violence, other variables like the role of external influence, Western culture, and influence of deprivation (as experienced by the alamagiris – beggars) in the violence can be used to research further on Northern Nigeria violence. Alternative variables emanating from participants' interviews can also be used to expand on possible solutions to the violence in Northern Nigeria.

References

Achebe, C. C. (2005, June 14). Professor Tam David-West in conversation [Interview]. *The Chinua Achebe foundation interview series Nigeria: A meeting of the minds.* Retrieved from http://nigeriaworld.com/feature/publication/chidi-achebe/061405.html

Adeoti, E. O., & Oaniyan, S. B. (2014). Ethnicity and national integration in Nigeria: A historical overview. *International Journal in Management and Social Science, 2*(2), 104-120. Retrieved from http://ijmr.net/wp-content/uploads/2014/02/Paper-5.pdf

Atofarati, A. A. (1992). *The Nigerian civil war, causes, strategies, and lessons learnt.* Retrieved from http://www.africamasterweb.com/BiafranWarCauses.html

Avruch, K. (1998). *Culture and conflict resolution.* Washington, DC: United Institute of Peace Press.

Bacik, G. (2002). A discussion on ethnic identity. *Alternatives: Turkish Journal of International Relations, 1*(1). Retrieved from http://www.alternativesjournal.net/volume1/number1/bacik.htm

Bačová, V. (1998). The construction of national identity: On primordialism and instrumentalism. *Human Affairs, 8,* 29-43. Retrieved from http://www.humanaffairs.sk/full/hum198c.pdf

Bangura, Y. (1994). *The search for identity: Ethnicity, religion and political* violence (Occasional paper no. 6). World Summit for Social Development. Retrieved from http://www.unrisd.org/80256B3C005BCCF9/%28httpAuxPages%29/2744F97BFD59E76080256B64004FA25E/$file/OPWSSD6.pdf

Blagojevic, B. (2009). Causes of ethnic conflict: A conceptual framework. *Journal of Global Change and Governance, 3*(1), 1-25. Retrieved from http://202.154.59.182/ejournal/files/CausesofEthnicConflict.pdf

Brown, G. K., & Langer, A. (2010, March). *Ethnic diversity and economic instability in Africa: Policies for harmonious development: Conceptualizing and measuring ethnicity* (JICA-RI Working Paper No. 9). Retrieved from http://jica-ri.jica.go.jp/100330%20wp%2009.pdf

Central Bank of Nigeria. (n.d.). *About CBN – Past and present governors.* Retrieved from http://www.cenbank.org/aboutcbn/allgovernors.asp

Chidi, I. (n.d.). *Nigeria's religious and cultural conflict.* Retrieved from http://www.google.com/url?sa=t&rct=j&q=&esrc=s&source=web&cd=1&ved=0CCUQFjAA&url=http%3A%2F%2Fweb.stanford.edu%2Fclass%2Fe297a%2FNigeria%27s%2520Religious%2520and%2520Cultural%2520Conflict.doc&ei=jp0UVJOAN8ymyATNvoDgBg&usg=AFQjCNFaAikCjyGNju7x5skeITc8e47xDA&bvm=bv.75097201,d.aWw&cad=rja

Ciboh, R. (2014). Newspaper inquest into Tiv-Jukun conflict 2001: An analysis of ethnic inequality and domination in contemporary Nigeria. *New Media and Mass Communication, 21,* 40-49. Available from http://iistejournalupdate.blogspot.com/2014/03/new-media-and-mass-communication-2014.html

Creswell, J. W. (2007). *Qualitative inquiry and research design: Choosing among five approaches* (2nd ed.). Thousand Oaks, CA: Sage Publications.

Ejiogu, E. C. (2013). Chinua Achebe on Biafra: An elaborate deconstruction. *Journal of Asian and African Studies, 48*(6), 653-670. doi:10.1177/0021909613506457

Ezeibe, C. C (2009). Inter-religious conflicts and crisis of development in Nigeria: Who benefits? *Society for Research and Academic Excellence, 1.* Retrieved from http://www.academicexcellencesociety.com/inter_religious_conflicts.html

136

Falana, F. (2015, January 17). Corruption: A state policy under Babangida. *NationalIssues posted by OpinionNigeria.* Retrieved from http://www.opinionnigeria.com/corruption-a-state-policy-under-babangida-by-femi-falana

Federal Judicial Service Commission. (2015). *List of chief justices of Nigeria.* Available from http://fjsconline.org/

Geertz, C. (1963). The integrative revolution: Primordial sentiments and civil politics in the new states. In C. Geertz (Ed.), *Old societies and new states: The quest for modernity in Asia and Africa* (pp. 105-157). New York: The Free Press of Glencoe. Retrieved from http://faculty.washington.edu/charles/562_f2011/ Week%2010/Geertz%20The%20Integrative%20Revolution.pdf

Global Security. (2014). *Nigerian Army order of battle* [Data]. Retrieved from http://www.globalsecurity.org/military/world/nigeria/army-orbat.htm

Harris, P., & Reilly, B. (Eds.). (1998). *Democracy and deep-rooted conflict: Options for negotiators.* Stockholm: International IDEA.

Human Rights Watch. (2002). Military revenge in Benue: A population under attack. *Journal of Human Rights Watch, 14*(2). Retrieved from http://www.hrw.org/sites/default/files/reports/Nigeria0402.pdf

Infoplease. (2015). Infoplease atlas – Africa. Retrieved from http://www.infoplease.com/atlas/africa.html

International Crisis Group. (2010, December 20). *Northern Nigeria: Background to conflict* (Africa Report No. 168). Retrieved from http://www.crisisgroup.org/en /regions/africa/west-africa/nigeria/168-northern-nigeria-background-to-conflict.aspx

Iro, C. (2014, February). Androcentrism: Gender role and feminism in Igbo cultural practices. Paper presented at African Work Group in Humanities and Social Sciences, Nova Southeastern University, Davie-Fort Lauderdale, FL.

Irobi, E. G. (2005, May). *Ethnic conflict management in Africa: A comparative case study of Nigeria and South Africa*. Retrieved from http://www.beyondintractability.org/casestudy/irobi-ethnic

Ismayilov, G. G. (2000). Ethnic conflicts and their causes. *Khazar Journal of Humanities and Social Sciences, 3*(4), 50-51.

Kaufman, E. (n.d.). *The power of ethnicity?: The geographic limits to modernist theories of intra-state violence*. Retrieved from http://www.sneps.net/NNE/1-1-The%20Power%20of%20Ethnicity.pdf

Mauthner, M., Birch, M., Jessop, J., & Miller, T. (Eds.). (2002). *Ethics in qualitative research*. London: Sage Publications.

Mudimbe, V. Y. (2013). Reading *There was a country*: A personal history of Biafra. *Journal of Asian and African Studies, 48*(6), 671-682. doi:10.1177/0021909613506487

Mustapha, A. R. (2004, March). *Ethnic structure, inequality and governance of the public sector in Nigeria* (UNRISD report). Retrieved from http://www.afrimap.org/english/images/documents/UNRISD%20Nigeria%20Mustapha.pdf

Nigeria. (2007). In *Worldmark encyclopedia of nations*. Retrieved from http://www.encyclopedia.com/doc/1G2-2586700117.html

Nigerian Army. (2014). *Nigerian army almanac*. Nigeria: Nigerian Army.

Njoku, C. I. (2013). A paradox of international criminal justice: The Biafra genocide. *Journal of Asian and African Studies, 48*(6), 710-726. doi:10.1177/0021909613506453

Nossiter, A. (2015, January 23). Beleaguered, Nigerians seek to restore a General to power. *New York Times*. Retrieved from http://www.nytimes.com/2015/01/24/world/africa/muhammadu-buhari-nigeria-election.html?_r=0

Oganesyan, M. (2009). *Constructing and deconstructing histories: The ethicity factor*. Retrieved from caucasusedition.net/wp-content/uploads/2010/06/Oganesyan_Final1.pdf

Ogbeidi, M. M. (2012). Political leadership and corruption in Nigeria since 1960: A socio-economic analysis. *Journal of Nigeria Studies, 1*(2), 1-25. Retrieved from http://www.unh.edu/nigerianstudies/articles/Issue2/Political_leadership.pdf

Okpanachi, E. (2012). *Ethno-religious identity and conflict in Northern Nigeria: Understanding the dynamics of Sharia in Kaduna and Kebbi states* (IFRA-Nigeria e-Paper No. 7). Retrieved from http://www.cetri.be/IMG/pdf/Okpanachi_2010.pdf

Olu-Adeyemi, L. (2006, February 15). *Ethno-religious conflicts and the travails of national integration in Nigeria's fourth republic*. Retrieved from http://www.dawodu.com/adeyemi3.htm

Onwuka, A. (2014, November 4). North: Igbo are not the problem. *Punch Magazine*. Retrieved from http://www.punchng.com/opinion/north-igbo-are-not-the-problem/

Pantazopolous, P. (1995). *Secessionist movement: An analytical framework* (Honors thesis). Retrieved from OpenSIUC database. (Paper No. 183)

Pew Research Center. (2011, December 19). *Religion and public life: Christian population in numbers by country* [Table]. Retrieved from http://www.pewforum.org/2011/12/19/table-christian-population-in-numbers-by-country/

Saldaña, J. (2009). *The coding manual for qualitative researchers*. London: Sage Publications.

Sampson, I. T. (2012). Religious violence in Nigeria: Casual diagnoses and strategic recommendations to the state and religious communities. *African Journal on Conflict Resolution, 12*(1), 103-134.

Shibru, D. (2009). Ethnic conflict in East Africa: An over view of causes and consequences. *Journal of Research in Arts and Education, 2*(4), 16-27. Retrieved from http://www.abhinavjournal.com/images/Arts_&_Education/Apr13/3.pdf

Stein, S. A. (2011). Competing political science perspectives on the role of religion in conflict. *Politorbis, 52-2*. Retrieved from http://www.css.ethz.ch/publications/pdfs/Politorbis-52-21-26.pdf

Stepaniants, M. (n.d.). *Ethnicity and religion*. Retrieved from http://www.dartmouth.edu/~crn/crn_papers/Stepaniants2.pdf

Teniola, E. (2014, April 24). Defence: From Ribadu to Gusau. *Punch Magazine*. Retrieved from http://www.punchng.com/opinion/defence-from-ribadu-to-gusau/

Tong, R. (2009). Explaining ethnic peace: The importance of institutions. *Res Publica – Journal of Undergraduate Research, 14*(1), 61-75. Retrieved from http://digitalcommons.iwu.edu/cgi/viewcontent.cgi?article=1144&context=respublica

United States Department of Justice. (2014, March 5). U.S. freezes more than $458 million stolen by former Nigerian dictator in largest kleptocracy forteiture action ever brought in the U.S. *Justice News*. Retrieved from http://www.justice.gov/opa/pr/us-freezes-more-458-million-stolen-former-nigerian-dictator-largest-kleptocracy-forfeiture

Universe on Web. (2011). *Niger River*. Retrieved from http://www.universeonweb.com/earth/earthriver/nigerriver.htm#.VUGElpMXGHQ

Weir, N. (2012). *Primordialism, constructivism, instrumentalism and Rwanda*. Retrieved from http://www.academia.edu/1526597/Primordialism

Willis, J. (2007). *Foundations of qualitative research: Interpretive and critical approaches*. Thousand Oaks, CA: Sage Publications.

Wimmer, A. (1997). Who owns the state? Understanding ethnic conflict in post-colonial societies. *Nations and Nationalism, 3*(4), 631-665. doi:10.1111/j.1354-5078.1997.00631.x

Yin, R. K. (1989). *Case study research: Design and methods* (Rev. ed.). London: Sage Publications.

Zeleke, B., & Abate, D. (2005, October). Inter-state ethnic conflict resolution strategies: Lessons to overcome ethnic conflicts in Ethiopia. In the *OSSREA Proceedings of the Second National Workshop of the Ethiopian*. Addis Ababa, Ethiopia. Retrieved from http://www.ossrea.net/index.php?view=article&catid=91%3 Aethiopia&id=272%3Ainter-state-ethnic-conflict-resolution-strategies&format=pdf&option=com_content

Appendix C: Maps

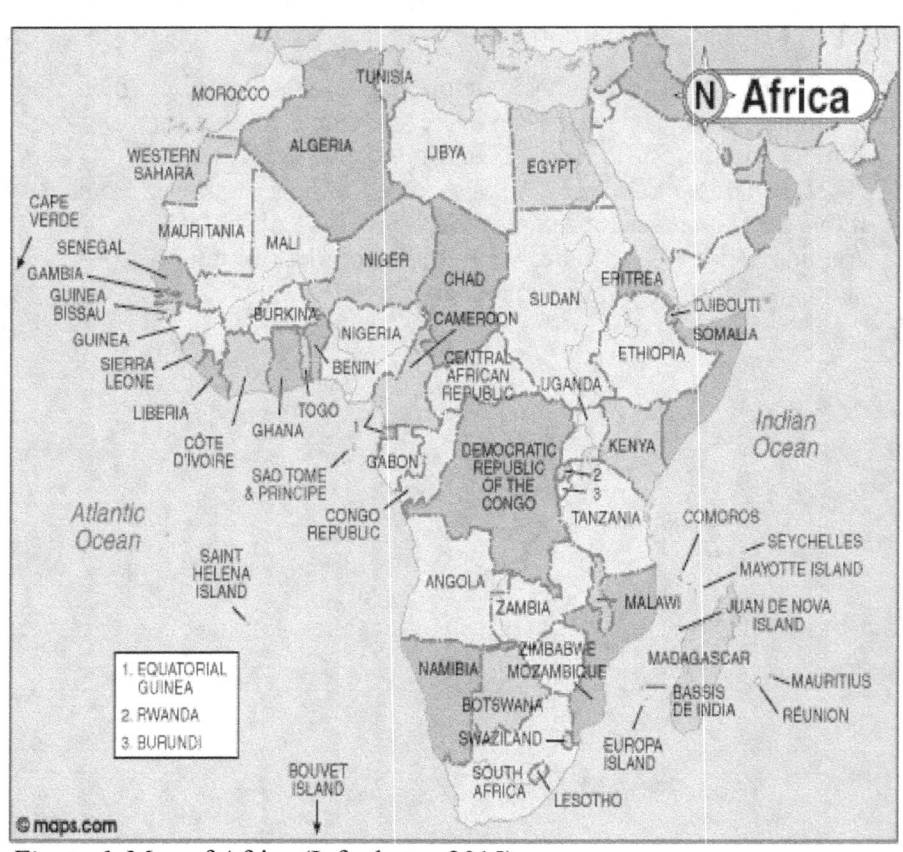

Figure 1. Map of Africa (Infoplease, 2015).

Figure 2. Map of Nigeria indicating countries within the Upper/lower Niger Basin (Universe on Web, 2011).

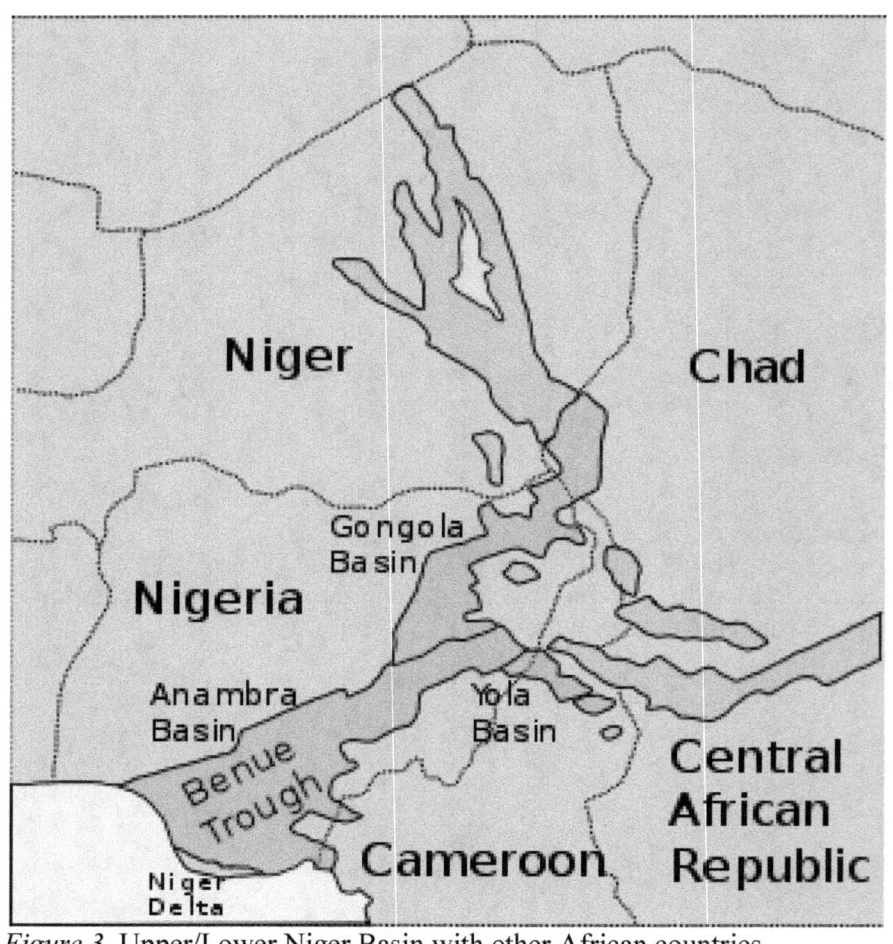

Figure 3. Upper/Lower Niger Basin with other African countries.

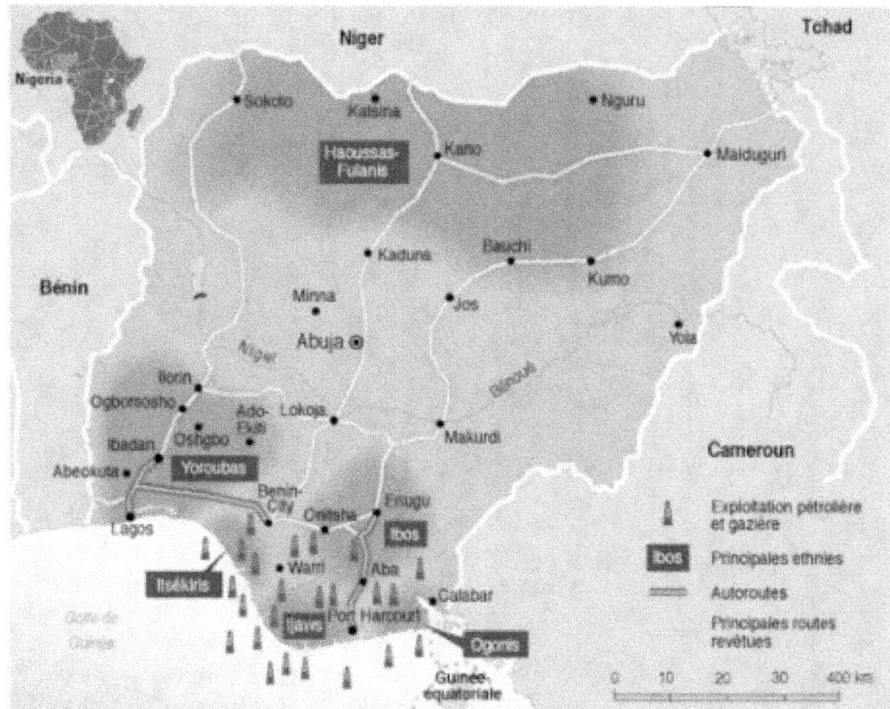

Figure 4. Map of Nigeria with cities in each region.